Waking Up
Bees

Be patient toward all that is unsolved
        in your heart and . . .
    try to love the questions themselves. . . .
Do not now seek the answers, which
        cannot be given you
    because you would not be able to live them.
And the point is, to live everything.
    Live the questions now.
Perhaps you will then gradually, without
        noticing it,
    live along some distant day into the answer.
                            Rainer Maria Rilke

Waking Up Bees

STORIES OF
LIVING
LIFE'S
QUESTIONS

JERRY DAOUST

Saint Mary's Press
Christian Brothers Publications
Winona, Minnesota

Short Fiction Books from Saint Mary's Press

Waking Up Bees
STORIES OF LIVING LIFE'S QUESTIONS

Mountains of the Moon
STORIES ABOUT SOCIAL JUSTICE

Genuine recycled paper with 10% post-consumer waste.
Printed with soy-based ink.

The quotation on page 2 is from *Letters to a Young Poet,* revised edition, by Rainer Maria Rilke, translated by M. D. Herter Norton (New York: W. W. Norton and Company, 1954), page 35. Copyright © 1954 by W. W. Norton and Company.

The publishing team included Barbara Allaire, series editor; Stephanie Hanson, development editor; Rebecca Fairbank, copy editor; Laurie Geisler, production editor and typesetter; Proof Positive/Farrowlyne Associates, Inc., front cover designer; Barbara Bartelson, back cover designer; Stephan Nagel, art director; pre-press, printing, and binding by the graphics division of Saint Mary's Press.

Printed in the United States of America

Printing: 9 8 7 6 5 4 3 2 1

Year: 2007 06 05 04 03 02 01 00 99

ISBN 0-88489-527-0

Contents

All Passages by Water Lead Home

L ook, Jim! It's more cool bovine scenery," Annie, who had just taken over driving, said cheerfully. I glanced up from the map I was studying (being in the navigator's seat) and Zoe popped up in the back where she had been curled up on sleeping bags and pillows, trying to catch forty winks.

"Moo, moo, little cows," Annie said. "Moo, moo."

"Since when are there cows in South Carolina?" Zoe said, pulling her black stocking cap up over her eyes. She was dying of cancer, and her hair hadn't grown back since she stopped chemotherapy. Back in Minnesota it was the middle of a winter so cold it would make the snot in your nose freeze solid, so she wore lots of hats. The black stocking cap was the warmest, but it made her look like a mobster. Fortunately, when she went to public places she wore a black beret, which at least made her look intellectual. "I thought South Carolina was known for peaches," she said.

"No, that's Georgia," I said. "Haven't you ever heard that song, 'My Georgia Peach'?"

"Is that by the Smashing Pumpkins?" Zoe asked, to be silly—she knew better.

Zoe knew all kinds of music. She could even sing operas by heart. She had sung *La Traviata* all the way through the deep blue shades of Missouri landscapes the night before, to keep awake at the wheel.

"Pumpkins are the official fruit of Indiana," Annie said.

"This car smells like pumpkins," I said, because it had that funky smell that comes with long trips—Doritos, stale pop and stale breath, ripe fruit, and sweat. We'd been on the road almost twenty-four hours straight with no sleep. That's the only way to travel, though, when you're in college and too poor for airplanes and motels, and too hungry for the road to let mere poverty stop you from getting on it and flinging yourself as far down it as you can. What else did God make all-night restaurants like Denny's and Perkins and Happy Chef for?

I was trying to figure out where we were, but I couldn't match up the little two-lane highway we were on with the map. That we were lost didn't surprise me, since we were penetrating foreign territory—none of us had been to the Deep South before, and it seemed to hold us as enchanted as newborn infants wide-eyed at a new world: all the kudzu hanging from the trees like green veils. The old barns weathered down to gray wood, listing to the side like sinking ships.

The round, warm vowels of the language. The decades-old Coca-Cola machines at small-town gas stations that gave us real glass bottles. The Civil War monuments littering the landscape everywhere.

I gave up on the map and folded it up. "Well, children, I think we're lost," I announced. "Maybe we should ask for directions."

Annie peered out from under her ever-present baseball cap at the sun. "Nah, as long as we're headed generally in the right direction, we'll hit the ocean eventually," she said. "Life is so much more interesting when you don't know where you're going, right?" She gave me a wicked look.

She was being sarcastic. During the night we'd fallen into a long, serious conversation about what we'd do after we graduated from college in a mere three months. None of us had a clue. You don't just go to the registration office and sign up for the rest of your life; there's no course syllabus or class requirement. Just time and space stretching out before you like a blank canvas or an empty page. What do you do with all of that? We felt like birds getting pushed out of the nest, or little kids getting thrown in the deep end of the pool: fall or fly, sink or swim.

"It scares me witless," Annie had said.

"Well, look at it this way," I'd told her philosophically, "not knowing where you're going in life makes it more interesting."

"Ha," she said. "I'll remember to use that on my parents next time they ask me what my plans are. Oh, and the bank I got my loans from, too. 'Isn't this interesting?' That's what I'll tell them when I default on the loan. Thanks, Jim."

It was Zoe who had suggested the trip in the first place, bringing it up late one night at the university newspaper where we had all toiled together for the past four years. We always had interesting conversations there, about relationships and politics and art and religion, especially on the late nights when we were all a little wired from too much coffee and pizza. We'd been talking about the journey of life or something, and Zoe said we should go on a real journey, and when that got our attention, she said she wanted to see the ocean since she had never seen it before.

"It's on my list of things to do before I die, seeing the ocean is," she'd said.

"You are not going to die," I told her. Zoe had a strong streak of melodramatic romanticism, which I figured came from writing too much poetry. "You are twenty-one years old."

"You've never seen her driving," Annie deadpanned without even looking up from her computer screen.

Of course, wouldn't you know Zoe was diagnosed with cancer later that year. How ironic. At the newspaper we joked about it; our strategy was to keep her spirits up by being lighthearted instead of all heavy and serious. But then her hair fell out, and she kept getting thinner and paler, until all that shaped her face was her bony skull, and we stopped talking about it altogether. But we made very sure she got to go on her trip to the sea.

Now that we were within a few minutes' drive of the ocean, Zoe was getting all hyper about it.

"I personally don't see what the big deal is," I said. "It's just a lot of water, like any of the lakes you see lying around back home, except so big you can't see the other side."

"No," Zoe said. "The ocean is the birthplace of all life on earth, including our own species. It's like the womb for the whole biosphere. There's something in us that longs to return to the sea."

I rolled my eyes. "Not me. I hate swimming. I hate taking baths, even."

"Return to the sea," Zoe continued, not listening to me (as usual). "Think of all those people who didn't make it across. I'll bet there's enough of them down there to make a whole country of drowned people."

"Eww," Annie said.

"My great-great-grandma was only nineteen when she came over," Zoe said. "Of course, she had to come, because otherwise she would have starved. It was the great potato famine in Ireland that made her come. Our country is populated with the descendants of all those millions of people who risked their lives coming over the ocean, to a place they'd never seen before, to make new lives." Zoe was silent for a long moment, resting her chin on the back of the car seat. "The water giveth life, and it taketh life," she said.

"Amen," Annie said, nodding.

"We'll get some salt-spray-scented air into you, Jim, and that'll cure you," Zoe said. "You'll see the poetry of the ocean."

When we got to the empty parking lot near the state park beach, it was a lot cooler, especially with the strong wind. We put our winter coats on. Grassy sand dunes blocked our view of the water. Zoe charged ahead, slipping in the sand occasionally. When she got to the top, she let out a whoop.

"Bonzai!" she yelled, and disappeared down the other side.

"She's not going swimming—is she?" I asked Annie, but she was already running after Zoe.

When I got to the top of the dune, I saw that Zoe wasn't going to run into the ocean after all. She'd taken off her shoes and was cautiously walking out where waves slid across the flat sand like tongues, leaving it so glassy-wet that I could see her reflection. Annie took a picture of Zoe ankle-deep in the water.

From the top of the dune, I looked out over the empty water, which was a sort of steel-blue color interrupted by flecks of white all the way out to the flat horizon. There weren't any boats or islands or anything out there. It was as forlorn as a desert, except of course there was all that water. And under the water, a whole world of millions of strange living things, and un-explored mountains and plains, and the shipwrecks of people who hadn't made it to the other end of the ocean. Walking along the beach, Zoe and Annie looked so small compared to the vastness of half the world stretching out behind them.

We pulled blankets and sleeping bags and food and Zoe's boom box out of the car and set up headquarters on the beach. We were planning to spend the night there, sleeping under the stars. There was no one else to bother us, except some gulls that Annie encouraged by tossing pieces of stale rolls out onto the sand, which attracted even more gulls. Pretty soon it looked like a scene from *The Birds,* there were so many gulls hovering around us.

We roamed the beach hunting for dry driftwood to make a fire with, and picked up some interesting seashells along the way. Zoe said she would make necklaces for her little sisters. For supper we made baked potatoes and vegetable stew over the fire, and brought out cheese and crackers and wine and avocados. Annie put on a tape of some jazz music, and we were in fine shape.

"I am warm and happy," Zoe said, eating a piece of avocado. She was wrapped up in a heavy wool blanket, and had a scarf wrapped around her head to keep the wind out of her ears. She smiled at us; Annie and I smiled back.

"You look like a babushka," Annie said.

The sun set behind us, orange-like, through the grasses of the dunes, and the sky above the water grew darker.

"Thank you for coming on this trip with me," Zoe said. "I could never have made the trip myself, without someone to take over the driving. Not that I would have wanted to—I mean, it wouldn't have been as much fun if I had traveled by myself."

"Of course, if you'd gone by yourself, you wouldn't have had to put up with Jim's annoying music," Annie said.

"Or Annie's snoring," I said.

"Shush," Annie said, slapping my arm with a mitten.

"No, it's better to travel together," Zoe said. "We need each other."

I leaned back to look at the darkening sky; I could make out the first stars there. I thought of *The Lion King*—stars being the souls of dead people or something like that. It was hard to comprehend Zoe as a star, though, a sharp little quiet piece of light. If she had her way, she'd be an exploding star, a supernova. Actually, if she had her way, she'd keep on living. Her pale presence so close on that beach—the blood and the breath moving in her like the waters of the ocean, her quick eyes, her songs, all the things she could spin with her hands and her heart—all of that burned with greater brightness than any of those faraway stars. And if a star fell from the sky, who would miss it? The universe is piled deep with them, and they all look alike from this far away. But when Zoe fell from the earth, there would be no getting her back. It made me mad at God, for taking away her life just as the most interesting part was coming up. I imagined God as someone who gives a kid a present, then smashes it to pieces.

"I never did like *The Lion King*," I said, breaking the long silence.

"What?" Annie said, frowning as if I'd sworn or spoken some blasphemy.

"So now that we're here at the edge of the ocean, what do we do?" I asked, to change the subject.

"If I had a boat, I would sail across it," Zoe said.

"I wouldn't," Annie said. "I'd be too afraid."

"Afraid of what?" Zoe asked blandly.

"Getting lost. Drowning."

"Drifting out there without any drinkable water for weeks on end is what you should be afraid of—a slow death like that," Zoe said. She poured herself more wine. "I should build a boat and sail across the ocean."

"Where would you go?" I asked.

"You can go almost anywhere by water," Zoe said. "Where to begin? I would go to the island of Pohnpei, where the yams grow ten feet long and the grasshoppers get as big as chickens, and the schoolchildren use giant pandanus leaves for umbrellas. In the 1800s, whaling ships stopped going there for provisions because so many men would desert that no one was left to sail the ships home.

"I would go to Glacier Bay to climb blue mountains of ice at the height of summer, when the sun never sets. I would take my boat to India, where I would learn to play the sitar. Maybe I would devote my life to teaching poor children in Calcutta to read and write Bengali.

"No, I would compete in the America's Cup sailing race without officially entering. Or maybe I would sail to Venice, where the cats own the city because there are no cars to run them over, and I could sing opera on the Bridge of Sighs. I would make friends with stamp collectors everywhere I went, and send postcards to all of them from every country I visited. And there's all of the South American coast, too, which is much closer to here. I could go to the Galapagos Islands and ride giant turtles for fun, or study new plant species and discover a cure . . ."

She pulled up short, as if she hadn't meant to bring that subject up with us—but how could we not think about it, as she sat there listing all those things she would never do? In the awkward silence, we heard the ocean breathe. She looked up at us. Her eyes were so big in her pale face, lit in several water-colored shades of yellow by the fire. She smiled like a ghost.

"The good thing about dying from cancer is that, in the good moments, it wakes you up more alive than most people ever are in a lifetime. God scatters us across the earth like so many mustard seeds, hoping we'll live the abundant life. God puts on this amazing dance act, this three-ring circus, this traveling magic performance"—she extended an open hand toward the water and the world beyond, "and what do we do? We all watch television and miss the show."

I had never heard Zoe give a speech like that before, and her earnestness embarrassed me, a little. I thought she might be slightly drunk from the wine. Or maybe being so close to death made her bold.

I saw tears on Annie's face. Zoe looked over, too, and she moved to cup Annie's cheeks with mittened hands.

"Don't cry," Zoe said. "Not for me. I know where I'm going. Just because you can't see to the other end of the ocean doesn't mean there isn't another shore all ships come to, right? We look out across the water and we don't see it, but only because we can't see that far. But we don't believe anymore that if we sail over the horizon, we'll fall off the end of the earth. I can smell it, Annie, like sailors on a ship can smell land ahead in the dark. It's there."

She leaned forward a little and kissed Annie on the forehead. "Don't be afraid; God is with you. Be brave. Explore everything. And don't watch too much television."

"But I'll sure miss watching old reruns of *Friends*," Annie teased, smiling a little and pushing away the tears with the palms of her hands.

"Make real friends instead."

That night all of us huddled together in our sleeping bags, trying to stay warm on that cold beach by the sea under the bright, bright moon. Zoe and Annie seemed to sleep soundly, but I kept drifting in and out of dreams. I think the rhythmic noise of the waves washing onto shore kept me awake, plus I worried that the tide would come in and drown us. Was the tide coming in or out tonight? I didn't know.

We were on the edge of new territory, each of us ready to go our own way—Annie and I out into what people referred to as the real world, Zoe out into another world entirely. The real "real world." The new world. A place I hoped Annie and I would come to at the end of our journey. We were on the edge of new territory, ready to step out, and nothing would be the same for us again.

Hush, hush, the waves seemed to say.

Zoe turned over and kicked me. "Move," she mumbled. "You're squashing me."

I made some more room, and fell asleep under the sound of their breathing, and that of the ocean.

Work of Mercy

I was doing my least favorite job, cleaning fish tanks, when the cockatoo named Snowflake escaped from his cage and took off flying around the store, terrorizing customers by diving at them in a frantic flurry of white feathers, like a small plane coming in for a really bad landing. I looked up from siphon-cleaning the tank gravel to see him descending onto the wild blond hair of a young boy who was doing his best to escape by rushing headlong down the aisle with his eyes and arms leading the charge faster than his feet could keep up. The boy broke sharply to the left around the shelves, knocked a display of squeaky chew toys into the middle of next week, and tackled his mom as his giggling little sister clapped her hands and called out, "Catch him! Catch him!"

Meanwhile, Snowflake flew headfirst into the display window at the front of the store, nicely punctuating the words Sullivan had written there in grease pencil: "FUR, FIN, AND FEATHER KRAZY DAZE SALE—BUY A FAITHFUL FRIEND, 20% OFF." Then he dropped like a rock behind the Purina display, flapping his wings against the glass. An old man standing by the cash register with two bags of Fur, Fin, and Feather Fantastic Finch Food adjusted his glasses and parted his lips. "Good lord," he murmured.

And there by the cockatoo cage stood Nina, her hand still on the door, staring at me solemnly from a pale face framed by her straight red hair. She looked like she might cry, but she didn't, she didn't at all. I pushed past her and went to the window. The bird was there in a corner, white as ivory and as wild as the jungle. He cocked his head and blinked a pearly black eye at me, ruffling his feathers angrily.

"Geez, Nina," I yelled, turning to grab a large towel from under the counter. The customers looked embarrassed; the kids' mother hustled them toward the door.

"Troy," Nina said hotly, taking a step forward. "He's going to die if you put him back in that cage." Her hand on the cage trembled.

For a moment, but only for a moment, I was too surprised to respond. "Unbelievable," I finally managed. "Who died and made you the pet police? He's not your bird, Nina—he's Sullivan's. What right do you have to let go someone else's fourteen-hundred-dollar bird? It's stealing."

"So killing is better than stealing?" she retorted, but I turned away from her eyes and held the towel loosely in my hands, raising it above Snowflake, moving slowly so I'd do it right the first time. Out of the corner of my eye I could see the wide pink mouth of the boy howling as his mother pushed him out the door. The cold washed into the store and over us, and Snowflake perked up, smelling freedom in the air. He stepped forward and lifted his wings.

It's not fair that there is never enough time to make the most important decisions, like the split second when you realize you're about to crash and you have to decide which way to turn and there's no time to consider the consequences; and you know that if you make the wrong decision, you'll have to live with it, but there's no time, so you do what instinct tells you to do. And at that moment, even though I was thinking, Should I just let Snowflake go? there was no time to think it through; it all happened too quickly.

I was only doing what I had been trained to do. I'd started working at Fur, Fin, and Feather nearly four years before that moment with Snowflake, way back in the summer I turned fourteen. I remember the first thing Sullivan ever told me: "Nothing ever dies here."

Now everything dies, even I knew that, even when I was fourteen and didn't know much else about animals. Sullivan must have seen that I didn't believe him for a minute, because he slowly leaned over the counter, thrusting forward his ruddy, broad face with its dark eyes—curled his thick lips into a wry smile, and repeated what he had to say: "Nothing ever dies in this pet shop," he said, cocking a bushy eyebrow, "because from now on your job is going to be to keep them alive. You're going to give them food when they're hungry; you're going to give them water when they're thirsty; you're going to give them a nice, clean cage to live in. You're going to be just like their mama. Okay?"

Heck, I would've tucked them in, read them a bedtime story, and kissed them good night to get that job, because what kid wouldn't want to work in a pet store? And Fur, Fin, and Feather was no ordinary pet store—not like Pets! Pets! Pets!, the sanitized corporate chain store at the mall. On Saturday mornings before the store opened and Sullivan got there, it was as raucous as Noah's ark. I would let the kittens, puppies, rabbits, ferrets, and whatever else was handy out of their cages, and they would chase one another all around the floor. I'd put the baby cockatiels up on the cash register, where they would cock their heads thoughtfully and practice flapping their wings. It smelled like Noah's ark, too, a rich blend of all the fur, dog food, exotic bird seed, fishy water, feather dander, and dirty cages, plus the smoke from Sullivan's cigarettes. On hot summer days, it could knock you out.

Animals died, of course; you couldn't help that. The ones that did I threw in the dumpster out back before any of the customers saw them and got upset. You didn't want someone shopping for fifty bucks' worth of tropical fish to find any floaters.

"It's bad for sales," Sullivan said.

It was good work. By my senior year of high school, I'd decided that it was better work than going off to college for four more years of school. I didn't know what I wanted to do with the rest of my life anyway—the "Choosing Your Career" handout we got at school gave me headaches with all its choices. My parents were skeptical until I pointed out that I would just be wasting their money switching majors all the time. When I put it that way, they agreed that maybe it would be better for me to take some time off from school.

I don't know whether God nudges things around in our life to get us going in the right direction, but what I had planned isn't what happened. Just as I thought I had everything all set, the rug got pulled out from under me—and Nina was the one doing the pulling. I had never really paid much attention to Nina and probably never would have if she hadn't shown up in class one day wearing a straw hat, which of course Mr. Huber told her to take off. When she wouldn't, he snatched it from her head, on top of which was a little white mouse that jumped off and scurried under the radiator as soon as everyone started laughing and screaming. Nina, who was never known for saying much, started crying—partly because Mr. Huber was yelling at her, partly because half the class was going into mock hysterics, and partly because she couldn't find her mouse.

Before I knew what I was doing, I was down on my hands and knees, peering under the radiator. "Have you ever smelled a dead mouse?" I asked Mr. Huber when he started yelling at me to get back in my seat. Mr. Huber said no, he hadn't.

"His name is Gordo. It means 'fatso' in Spanish," Nina offered helpfully, as if I could get the mouse to come out by calling its name. That got the whole class laughing again. Then I cornered Gordo and grabbed him by the tail. Nina dropped him into her hat, and Mr. Huber told her to put it in her locker until after school.

"Uh, you might want to wash your hair while you're at it," one of the guys called out. People snickered.

Nina passed me on her way out the door. "Thank you," she murmured, her freckles burning bright red. Nina would blush if she was even called on in class, which may have been why she never talked to anyone, except for a couple close friends, and no one ever talked to her. She was as out of place among the rest of us as someone born in the wrong century, or a foreigner who doesn't know the local language. So it wasn't like people intentionally ignored her; it was more that, after getting used to her quietness, they had just stopped seeing her.

I had gone after the mouse more for its sake than Nina's, but it turned out they were a two-for-one package. She showed up at the store that afternoon with Gordo the mouse cradled in her hands, wanting to give him to me to sell to a good home through Fur, Fin, and Feather.

"You mean after all that trouble at school, you're going to give him away?" I teased.

"Well," she said, glancing away at the aquariums. "Well, my dad says he's going to flush him down the toilet if I don't get rid of him."

"Oh," I said lamely. "Is that why you took him to school?"

She nodded. "I was hiding him in my room, but he chewed out of the cardboard box and got into the kitchen." There was an awkward pause as she stared fiercely at the angel fish. "Dad got really mad. He would've stepped on him, but I got to Gordo first and promised I wouldn't bring him back into the house. So I thought you could slip him in with your other white mice."

"Nina," I said as gently as I could, "we sell those mice for people to feed to their snakes."

This didn't go over very well. She brought her hand to her throat and her face went white—in fact, she looked like a little mouse in a snake cage herself. I tried pointing out that snakes have to eat, too, but she was unconvinced.

"Don't you have any compassion?" Nina asked, her voice squeaking a little.

In the end, I put her mouse in a separate cage away from the others, in the back of the store. We made a sign for it: "FRIENDLY PET MOUSE—NOT FOR SNAKES." Almost every day after school, Nina would come check on Gordo and feed him bits of cheese. She would put him on her shoulder and take a tour of the store, stopping in front of every cage and aquarium to peer in at the animals there.

About that time Sullivan got back from his annual overseas vacation, where he usually bought some exotic animal to sell at the shop. This time he brought a sulfur-crested cockatoo back from Hong Kong. Normally it was illegal to sell cockatoos there, but Sullivan explained this one descended from a flock in the downtown business district that had gone wild when they were set free from the city aviary during World War II. (Someone thought they'd be eaten by the invading Japanese soldiers.) The birds had become such pests—breaking branches off trees and stealing fruit from street vendors— that the government decided to trap and sell them. Sullivan liked this bird so much that he named it Snowflake (for its white feathers) and decided to make it the store's mascot: a decoration for the front window to draw in more customers.

Nina was there when Sullivan began breaking in Snowflake. She observed him silently from several steps away, gently stroking the mouse on her shoulder with one finger. Sullivan pulled on heavy leather gloves, peered into the kennel he had been keeping the bird in, and regarded him a moment. The bird, crouched low on its perch, gazed back at Sullivan warily, ready to fly—had there been anywhere to fly. Sullivan opened the cage, and the cockatoo raised his yellow crest, puffed out his feathers, lifted his wings, opened his hooked beak, and hissed like a snake. Slowly Sullivan reached in, and Snowflake exploded, banging his wings against the metal walls of the cage and lunging forward with his beak to bite off Sullivan's hand, which Sullivan pulled back very quickly, swearing. Fluffy little white feathers floated in the air.

"Should've named him Blizzard," I commented. Sullivan gave me a dark look.

The parakeets in the large flight cage, normally as noisy as a lunchroom full of first graders, were suddenly quiet like church, watching us. I held my breath as Sullivan extended his hand into the cage again, this time with his fingers withdrawn into the palm of the glove. When Snowflake struck and clamped down on the empty leather fingers, Sullivan thrust his other hand into the cage and expertly grabbed the bird from behind the neck, so that he held its head between his thumb and forefinger. When the bird released the glove to squawk angrily, Sullivan reached under its belly with that hand and grabbed it, pinning down its wings.

He pulled the bird out and held it up to his face. "He thinks I'm going to have him for lunch—don't you, you big white chicken?" The cockatoo was still fighting, his claws grabbing at the air, his yellow crest raised like a spiked mohawk.

"Here, clip his wings while I hold him," Sullivan said, flipping the cockatoo onto its back on the counter. This is something we did all the time with the parakeets and cockatiels. I took a long pair of scissors and carefully extended one of Snowflake's wings.

Birds' wings are so light, I always worry that they will break in my hands.

"What are you doing?" Nina asked anxiously, not moving from where she stood.

"We're going to cut some of his feathers away so he doesn't go flying off," I explained.

"Don't worry, it doesn't hurt him—the part of the feathers I'm cutting is dead, like your hair."

"But he won't be able to fly . . ."

"That's the idea," Sullivan interrupted. "Let's get this over with, Troy."

I did, cutting away the bottom half of the primary feathers except for two at the tip of the wing. The white cuttings spun down to the floor like falling leaves. I moved around the counter to clip the other wing and noticed Nina's face—tragic, her eyes brimming with tears. I ignored that, turning to the job of clipping the wing.

When I had finished, Sullivan turned Snow-flake over and let go. Immediately he took off from the counter, flapping furiously, only to glide to the floor at Nina's feet.

"Oh!" she said, reaching down, but he took off again, making a short hop down the aisle.

Sullivan followed, easily cornering the bird and picking him up again. "He's still wild—we're going to have to work it out of him," he told me, carrying the bird into the back room. "This will be a good opportunity for you to learn to tame larger birds, Troy."

"I guess," I replied, looking after Nina, who had quietly slipped out the door. Strange kid, I thought.

Taming the cockatoo turned out to be more of a challenge than Sullivan thought, though, because after that day Snowflake wouldn't do anything at all. When Sullivan put his hands in the cage, Snowflake scampered into a corner and hissed, but otherwise—nothing. You could see his heart beating, he was so still. He didn't even move to eat, not even fresh fruit. After three weeks the only progress we had made was to make him molt prematurely, so that you could see large bald patches of pink skin. Sullivan moved his cage off the front counter and into the back. He laid off the physical training and tried playing Snowflake a continuous tape of other cockatoos' calls interspersed with a woman's voice that said, "Hello, pretty bird! Whatcha doin'?" but Snowflake might have been deaf for all the interest he showed in that.

"I might as well have bought a stuffed cockatoo. Would've saved me a grand or so," Sullivan muttered. "Actually, that's not a bad idea."

"Nina thinks he's depressed," I told Sullivan casually. "She thinks he'll never be tamed."

Actually she had been more explicit than that. She had been intensely interested in

Snowflake; I always seemed to find her standing very still in front of his cage, watching him sit just as still on his perch. Sometimes when she didn't know I was near, I heard her speaking to him softly— words of encouragement, I guess.

"God made a place for everything to be," she had said, hanging onto the cage with her fingers and staring in at Snowflake after I was done with him one day. "This isn't his place, and he knows it. Not like these dumb fish that swim in circles around their tiny aquariums all day waiting for their next meal, or even those kittens over there that were born in someone's house. Not like you." Her face flushed and she bit her lower lip.

"What do you mean by that?"

"You know this bird is going to die before it's ever tamed," she said slowly. "All he knows is flying wild. But you keep trying to force him to become something he's not—a showpiece, a pet, a puppet on a string, a gentle little snowflake." She looked away from Snowflake, and looked straight at me. "He doesn't know how to not be what he is, and you know that, so why are you killing him slowly like this?"

"Sullivan's the boss," I said. "It's not up to me."

"Are you afraid of him?" she asked. I thought, This angry-sounding girl can't be Nina.

"Look," I said, "I'm just doing my job, okay? I don't like it, either, but it's his animal and he's the boss."

She looked away.

"But you're probably right," I said. "I'll bring it up with Sullivan, okay? I know animals are important to you."

"They're the only living things I know that won't purposely hurt you," she said. "Not the way people will."

I couldn't stop thinking about what Nina had said, probably because she was right. I had taken the pet store job for the animals, because you didn't have to win a popularity contest to win an animal's friendship. What I wanted was to become an animal charmer, a second Saint Francis—not someone who beat animals into submission, like we were doing with Snowflake. So I tried making Sullivan see that the cockatoo wasn't going to be tamed, but he wouldn't hear it.

"I can't return him," he said wryly. "And I'm sure not going to send fourteen hundred dollars off into the bright blue sky. Tell her not to worry. We'll get him tamed; it's just going to take longer than I thought."

The next day as I cleaned the fish tanks I watched them swimming around aimlessly looking for their next meal on the surface, without a clue that their fifteen-gallon tank was not the ocean they were supposed to have been born into. As I stared at those mindless fish I saw the reflection of my face in the glass, seeming to float, ghostlike, among them; and the dusty shelves along the walls behind me, and the fluorescent lights on the ceiling, and the cash register on the counter.

"Stupid fish," I thought.

And it was at that moment that Nina decided to emancipate Snowflake from his cage: the little boy started screaming, and I saw Snowflake, flying—flying awkwardly, on feathers that had grown out just barely enough to keep him aloft in the air, but flying. And I went to see what was going on, and found Nina standing there by the cage, looking surprised at herself. I secretly wished for the boy to go running out the door with Snowflake right behind him, out into the cold where he would rise up to be lost in winter's white air. Instead he flew headfirst into the front window, and I found myself moving to put him back in his cage, wondering, Am I doing the right thing?

But as Snowflake lifted his wings, I let the heavy towel drop over him and then quickly wrapped his body in it, keeping well away from his sharp beak. In this shroud I carried him back to his cage, put him on the floor inside, and unwrapped the towel. He jumped away from me, beating his wings against the brass bars, and I closed the door.

Nina did not say a word. She lowered her eyes and did not look at me anymore. Part of me wanted to explain to her why I couldn't just let Snowflake go, how sometimes you have a responsibility to do things that you don't really want to do; but I couldn't find the right words, so I didn't say anything.

"Well, that was exciting," the man with the finch food said brightly.

The next Saturday I found Snowflake sitting dead at the bottom of his cage. I knew he was dead right away because his body was tipped slightly sideways, leaning up against the bars of the cage. I stared at him a moment, feeling a bitter satisfaction that Nina had been right. I thought of taking him out into the snow, but then I had a better idea. I took Snowflake's cage out front and put it on the counter for the customers to see.

"What the hell is this?" Sullivan demanded of no one in particular when he finally showed up. He stood over the cage looking down at Snowflake. A skinny kid stood by him, chewing gum and staring with obvious fascination.

"Looks like a dead bird to me," the kid said smartly.

I laughed, and I didn't stop when Sullivan glared at me. I was thinking of Snowflake flying around the store, trying to land on the customers. It hadn't seemed funny at the time, but now it reminded me of a picture in the children's Bible I used to have, a picture of the Holy Spirit descending as a white bird onto the Apostles, who were huddled together hiding in the upper room. And I wondered, had they been just as startled?

Sullivan looked surprised when I gave my two-week notice, and wanted to know why I was quitting.

"Um," I said, stalling. How could I explain to him my sudden realization that I didn't want to spend the rest of my life working in a pet store?

"I'm taking an internship at the Raptor Rehabilitation Center when I start at the university this fall," I said, making something up. "You know, that place where they help injured eagles and hawks get better so they can go back to the wild."

And who was to say I wouldn't do just that? I could already imagine myself holding those creatures, bringing them out under the wide sky, uncurling my hands from around their wings: I lift them up and let go, holding my arms outstretched as they circle away higher and higher; I watch them return to the place that God has made for them, knowing that I am in the place God has made for me.

Leaving Tijuana

One moment he had been fighting in a bar named Adelita's; the next, he was squinting up from his perspective on the ground as the boy who loomed above him offered pesos to a police officer, who made the money vanish.

The officer, the boy, the drunken brute that Lacey had been fighting, and the donkey painted with zebra stripes—all were lit in gaudy reds and purples by the light of the neon signs lining Coahuila Street. The boy had saved Lacey from spending the night in jail with the other drunk Americans. He had spoken softly to the stocky, stern-faced police officer, while the man who had removed Lacey from the bar to the street kept interrupting in a loud, slurred voice, waving his hands in the officer's face. But the boy had money.

"Aqui vienen a hacer lo que en los Estados Unidos no los dejan hacer," the officer reflected, gazing down at Lacey and shaking his head with a thin smile: *They come here to do what they cannot do in the United States.* Then he was gone, and so was the brute and

the few disappointed onlookers who had
gathered to watch the Anglo be hauled away.

The boy helped Lacey up to his feet and
directed him to the saddle on the donkey's
back, ignoring his incoherent protestations.
Lacey slumped forward and hugged the donkey's neck, the coarse hair of its mane pressing against his pale cheek. The boy took the
rope and clucked at the animal, softly calling, "Cholo! Cholo!"

They proceeded down the avenue, a little
parade for the late-night crowd. Teenage
boys called out from the second-floor ter-
races of the discos, and bands of loud young
men looked back over their shoulders as
they passed. Well-dressed, sober American
couples stood in a restaurant doorway and
stared; mariachi music blaring from inside
the establishment drowned out whatever
comment they made on the scene.

The boy and the donkey paused to wait for
the tide of beat-up taxicabs and cars from
California to part so they could cross the
street. A young girl with braided hair and an
oval face pressed her palm against Lacey's leg
and held some ragged-looking satin flowers
up to his face, the dregs of her day's work.
"Buy my stuff, mister," she insisted, her large
eyes dark and empty. "Give me money."

"I don't have any money," he rasped.
"Do I look like I have any money?" The

boy said something to her in Spanish and chased her away.

They passed into a quieter quarter of the city, where only the round moon lit their way. Lacey roused himself sufficiently to wonder just where he was being taken, but while trying to climb off the back of the burro, he fell into the street. The boy stopped and looked down at the American, who had closed his eyes and was curling up on the pavement. He sighed and consulted the donkey, but it only twitched its ears and stood there patiently, its eyes reflecting the moonlight.

In the morning Lacey found himself lying on blankets in a small one-room shack. Slits of orange sunlight filtered through cracks in the wall, which was an amalgamation of corrugated metal, wood pallets marked "SANYO," and cardboard. The tar-paper roof bowed downward, so that he had to stoop when he got up.

Lacey stood in the doorway, gripping the frame as a support against his dizzy head, and blinked at the new sun that hung over the horizon. The boy was squatting on the ground next to a small fire. He gravely nodded at Lacey and in broken English introduced himself as Alejandro Morales. Lacey

grunted through the phlegm in his throat and
stepped out to a crate set on its end in the dirt.
He sat there with his head hung low to
shield his eyes from the sun.

"Lacey Pruske," he said, taking in
Alejandro's brown face with its thin mustache and crooked teeth. In Spanish he
asked, "Do you have any coffee?" Alejandro
grinned at him as if to say, You must be kidding. He produced a cup instead, filling it
with tepid water from a large plastic jug.

Alejandro made tortillas smeared with
bean paste for breakfast, pushing the food
around on the skillet with a fork. Lacey
sipped at the water, swishing it around in his
mouth and spitting it out on the ground. He
took in the neighborhood, a collection of
hundreds of do-it-yourself shacks the size of
storage sheds set haphazardly on the slope of
a dusty brown hillside. There were no roads,
only footpaths interspersed with garbage,
and colorful laundry hanging on makeshift
clothes lines. The hillside overlooked the
Tijuana metropolis, from which a faint haze
rose through the slanting morning light.

Three small children sat in a line against
the wall of the neighboring house, watching
Alejandro and Lacey eat, and fiddling with
the tuner on an old radio. For a moment it
picked up a San Diego traffic report about
an overturned semi on the Coronado Bridge:

"If you're heading to the beach this morning," the DJ was saying, "this backup is going to make you lose your will to live." The children's mother poked her head out the door occasionally to check on them, but said nothing to Alejandro about the blond American tourist sitting with him. Lacey wondered whether the children begged for money downtown. As they ate they talked, relying mostly on Lacey's passable Spanish.

"You looked pretty bad last night, man," Alejandro said. "You kept trying to get off the donkey!"

"What donkey?" Lacey asked, touching his tender face. Dried blood matted his hair, and he smelled of urine. He rubbed his forehead and tried to remember how things had gone so wrong the previous night. He had been on the wrestling team in school, and thought he should have beaten the older man in the bar. Well, it didn't matter.

"Cholo, the donkey who took you here. You don't think I carried you all this way?" Alejandro grinned, gesturing across the hillside.

"Did you see my friends? Two guys, about my age . . . ?" Lacey asked. Alejandro shook his head somberly, and Lacey's embarrassed blue eyes dropped to the ground before him, then roved the horizon, squinting. His nostrils twitched at the foul aroma carried on the breeze rising gently from the land

below, and as he watched a man farther down
empty a bucket of dark water, he realized the
smell came from rills of raw sewage. It
seemed strange that this place could exist
just twenty miles south of the green lawns
and broad paved streets of San Diego, where
yesterday at this time he and Becky had
been roller blading in Belmont Park.

"You were lucky I came along when I did,
or you would be waking up with a hangover
in a jail cell. I thought of my wife when I saw
you in the street," Alejandro said, looking at
Lacey pointedly as he ate. "I remembered
your *novia,* and I thought of how happy you
were with her. How could I pass you by?"

"Wait," Lacey said. "How did you know
about Becky?"

"I took your picture," Alejandro said, "on
the donkey cart, several weeks ago."

Lacey remembered that. They had come
down for the weekend. He had dragged
Becky over to one of the carts where for five
dollars you could sit on a donkey painted with
stripes and have your picture taken in black
and white on an antique Kodak camera; the
print was made there in the street. Alejandro
had been assisting the old photographer, and
had told Becky that the animal was a half-
breed, a burro crossed with a zebra. She had
believed him until Lacey laughed.

"She wouldn't care what happened to me, since she broke up with me yesterday," Lacey said.

"Oh," Alejandro said. He stopped eating and stared at Lacey as if he were personally disappointed by the news. "Why did she leave you?"

"She said I drink too much," Lacey replied. And she would be feeling pretty justified if she knew that I had to be rescued from the gutter by a Mexican donkey cart assistant last night, he added to himself.

"You have a girlfriend?" he asked Alejandro, to change the subject.

"I have a wife and a son."

"You look young to have children."

"He's a small baby."

"You all live here?" Lacey said, because he couldn't imagine them all living together in the small shack in which he had woken up.

"No," Alejandro said, smiling faintly. "I would return home to Chichimequillas, return to my old job cutting leather at the shoe factory, before I let them live here. My children won't go begging in the streets."

"Then where do they live?"

Alejandro studied his hands. "They're waiting for me." He looked up. "In Chicago, with my brothers."

Lacey whistled low. "That's a long commute from Tijuana, brother."

Alejandro rose abruptly and took the dirty plates inside the shack and emerged again with sweet bread. He tore off a piece for Lacey and called the three children to him, giving some to each of them. They ate the bread carefully, watching Lacey with curiosity.

The mother stood in the doorway, arms folded across the front of her yellow dress.

"See, we share what we have with each other here," Alejandro said. "We are all poor, but at least no one starves. But soon I will be in the United States. I will wash dishes, like my brothers. They make"—he paused to think—"ten times as much money as at the shoe factory in Chichimequillas, maybe more. They have been sending money to my mother, so she can build a house. Things will be good," Alejandro said, smiling at the children, who smiled back, "as soon as I get across the border. This time, I will be too quick for *la migra.*"

The children laughed. "Like coyote," one said.

"Yes, like coyote," Alejandro said.

"I suppose I would leave, too, if I were you," Lacey said, rising to go. He was suddenly uneasy with the course of the conversation, and disturbed by the children watching him, as if they expected something from him. Time to get home, he thought. He wondered whether his car was still where he left it the night before. He felt around in his pockets for his keys and wallet, and was relieved to find he still had them.

"Is it true that in America children receive their own cars for their sixteenth birthday?" Alejandro asked, eyeing the keys.

"Uh—it depends," said Lacey, who had in fact driven down to Tijuana in a car given to him by his parents as a graduation present.

"Hey," Lacey said suddenly. "I owe you one. You hear stories about the jails down here, but I wasn't interested in finding out firsthand, you know what I mean? What do I owe you?" He pulled out his wallet, wondering how much it cost to bribe a police officer in Tijuana.

Alejandro rose. "Help me get across the border."

Lacey looked up abruptly, surprised. He tried to read the Mexican's quiet face, gauging whether he might actually be serious. His eyes were like those of the beggar girl the night before. Everywhere you turn here, Lacey thought, there's someone wanting something from you.

"You could hide me in the trunk of your car," Alejandro said.

"Well, that's illegal, you know," Lacey said. "I guess I don't need to tell you that."

"No," Alejandro said. "But bribing a police officer is illegal, too."

Lacey stood there stony-faced, arms folded across his chest. He knew Alejandro, he realized. He'd seen him more times than he could remember, on the news at night or in the morning paper. He was just another one of those crazy border-crossers who were always finding new ways to die crossing the line. They drowned in the ocean and got eaten by fish, or were raped and beaten to death by bandits hiding in the brush waiting for their careful footsteps like hunters wait for deer. Or they froze in the mountains of East County, the snow so deep it pulled off their shoes and socks. They dashed across I-5 carrying their children and got smashed by trucks; they led the border patrol on high-speed chases that ended in fiery car wrecks; they suffocated silently in the hot, black trunks of cars. You could get sick of hearing such stories. You could get to wishing they would just stay home and leave you alone. Yet still they came, all those desperate *polleros,* hoping for—what? Their own car?

Alejandro reached out and grabbed Lacey's arm. "Please," he said, speaking rapidly to make his case. "I spent all the money I saved in Chichimequillas to hire the smuggler to guide my wife and me across the border. But the border patrol found us, and I had to let them catch me so María could escape. They caught me in the tall brush.

The border patrol has glasses to see in the dark—they let me look through them. What chance do I have against men who can see in the dark, like ghosts? Without a smuggler, I will surely be caught again. It will take many more months for me to save enough money to hire another smuggler. I haven't ever seen my baby son, my child. You can have all the money I've saved—"

"I don't want your money. I want to go home," Lacey said abruptly, shaking off Alejandro's arm. He could see the hope drain from Alejandro's face. He took out his wallet again and found a twenty, which was all he had. He hoped it would be enough to appease Alejandro. He held it out. "Thank you for saving me. Now we're even."

The children, who had gotten all solemn-faced, watched the bill hanging over their heads in fascination. Alejandro sulked for a long moment, then reached out and took it with the tips of his fingers, folding it over and sliding it into his pocket.

"I'm going to work now," he said. "I will bring you back. *Vámonos.*"

Alejandro began to make his way down the hillside. Lacey followed, relieved. He looked back, and one of the children waved good-bye to him happily. He quickly looked away, but his gaze found no restful scene anywhere, only the eyes of more potential *polleros* watching him: a man smoking a cigarette on some steps, a woman hanging laundry, more small children playing with a ball and a dog in the dirt. All of their maddeningly placid faces seemed to ask a question of him. He imagined millions of them pressing up against that steel border fence, pounding against it with their fists, making an unceasing noise.

So he focused his eyes on Alejandro's back, and in his mind he answered their questioning faces with questions of his own: You think you would be happy if you had all I have? My carpeted floors, crystal wine glasses, ten-dollar-a-bottle shampoo, MTV? If that is where happiness comes from, then why do I come down here to get drunk with my friends and lie in your gutters?

They passed a little retaining wall that some-one had made of old tires stacked on top of each other to hold back the mud in the rainy season. Flowers were planted atop the tires—nasturtiums, geraniums, roses, and others that Lacey was at a loss to name but that spilled over their dusty containers in brilliant profusion.

Avenida Revolución was full of Saturday-morning activity, bustling with American families pushing strollers and anxious street vendors calling out to them to buy a taco, buy a blanket, buy a picture on a zebra donkey. Lacey found his car where he had left it the night before in the Zona Norte, and parted with Alejandro, who would go to the stable where Cholo was waiting patiently for him.

Although it was a Saturday, there were still long lines at the border. Above the gates a sign flashed: "Baja Cellular gives you the correct time: 8:34"—which was four minutes fast by Lacey's watch. Although he had come here the previous evening to defy Becky—to show her she couldn't tell him what to do— he had succeeded only in making himself feel more powerless. He couldn't wait to get through the border gate.

The air was heavy with exhaust fumes, and already hot. He turned on the radio, but there was nothing but loud commercials. He turned it off again. The *traperos* were out, moving among the cars, rags in hand. Lacey watched an old man dusting off a station wagon; the kids in the back were making silly faces against the window, watching the man with animated expressions. Like the kids back in the shanties, Lacey thought, but not like them at all—these kids were leaving. It suddenly occurred to him how easy it would have been to hide Alejandro in the trunk of his car, then drop him off some- where in San Diego. Give him a bus ticket to Chicago. He shut his eyes tight. Try not to think about it, he thought. But in his mind's eye he could only imagine Alejandro reunited with his wife and newborn son, and the joy in their faces.

"Mister, want your car dusted off?" One of the *traperos* had snuck up to Lacey's window, startling him: a smiling man in a straw hat and a Coca-Cola T-shirt. There was a boy with him who looked to be about eleven.

"I don't have any money," Lacey said, and this time it was true; he had given all of it to Alejandro.

"Please mister," the man persisted. "We have to get enough money to take my wife to the doctor. She's very sick. She has this enormous lump in her stomach, and she hurts a lot."

"I told you I don't have any money!" Lacey barked. There was no escaping the endless need of these people, he thought, suddenly feeling justified for refusing Alejandro. If he'd given in to Alejandro, he'd have to give in to these people too, and soon there would be no end to the needy banging at his door. They'd take everything he had, until he had nothing.

"We work very cheap," the boy offered. "Only a few coins. Change from the cracks of your car seats."

Lacey looked forward, his jaw tight, and gripped the steering wheel harder. Inexplicably, the line wasn't moving. The Baja Cellular correct time was 8:58, and they'd barely moved an inch. He looked around: a woman moved among the cars selling red roses. He had come to Tijuana to escape the emptiness he felt at home, but this place only seemed to magnify it. He was desperate to get away from it, to the other side of the gate, where the sense of emptiness would surely leave him.

"Fine," he said, and got out of the car, much to the surprise of the man and the boy. They stepped back, ready to run. "All you have to do is drive this to the other side of the border, see? I'll be waiting for you on the other side, and you can just walk back to Tijuana." He began walking toward the pedestrian bridge. "I'll get some cash from an ATM, and I'll pay you then, okay?" he called back to the man and the boy, who were looking at him dumbfounded, as if he'd gone loco. "In dollars. Okay?" The man nodded and waved him on.

A few minutes later, Lacey was at the pedestrian bridge, where there was no line. He was breathing hard. He felt as if he'd been freed from a trap.

A bored customs agent began asking the standard questions: "What is your country of origin? What is your mother's maiden name? Did you purchase anything during your visit?"

Lacey just stared at the customs agent, and then back at the cars. He was thinking of something else entirely.

"Sir," the agent was saying, raising his voice slightly. "Did you purchase anything while in Mexico?"

The man and the boy, being Mexican, wouldn't be able to get through the border. They'd be turned back . . . with the car.

"My car," Lacey said slowly. He swore.

"You purchased a car?" the border agent asked. "Then why—"

Lacey set off running, dodging through the lines of cars, jumping up now and then to see better. The lines were moving forward now— haltingly, but making decent progress. More border gates had opened with the shift change at nine o'clock. He stopped and scanned the lines, like someone lost in a parking lot.

"Looking for something?" a woman asked from a burgundy Ford Escort, her eyebrows arched above her mirrored sunglasses.

"I gave away my car," Lacey said, throwing up his hands. "Why'd I do that?"

The woman wrinkled her nose. "Out of the goodness of your heart, I'm sure," she said wryly. He saw how her sunglasses reflected a misshapen representation of him standing there. She rummaged through her purse. In a moment she rolled down her window far enough to stick her hand out at him.

"It's a little early to be drinking—or maybe you're just out really late? Ha ha. But anyway, here," she said. "Fare for the trolley back to San Diego," and she pulled ahead in the line, leaving Tijuana as Lacey stood there among the cars on the Mexican side of the border, staring at the dollar bills in his hand as if they might contain a message.

Waking Up Bees
and Other Tricks of Love

*W*e tore down the Winnie-the-Pooh wallpaper in my brother Christopher's bedroom last weekend as a present for his eighteenth birthday. I'm not kidding—that's what he asked for. He'd always liked Pooh growing up, but now he was saying he wasn't a baby anymore, and Winnie-the-Pooh was for babies. So Mom and Dad bought him new curtains and new bedsheets, and I helped with the wallpaper, because I was home from school for a long weekend.

It was sort of weird, ripping down those pictures of Pooh with his head stuck in a honey jar and bees flying all around. I actually felt kind of sad about it. I guess who wouldn't feel guilty tearing apart Eeyore and Piglet and Tigger, too—but it was weird because growing up, Christopher's babyish room was one of the things about him that kept me in perpetual mortal embarrassment. That was partly why I wouldn't bring friends over to the house, that and the way he would always bug us, hanging around wanting to be doing whatever me and my friends did.

Even way back when we were little I remember the kids at school teasing me about him. You know how mean kids are: "Ooo, don't touch Lily, she's got retard germs from her brother!" Stuff like that. It made me cry until I learned that most useful grade school rhyme: "I am rubber and you are glue, whatever you say bounces off me and sticks on you!"

Of course after a while I got smart and just blew them off. But it wasn't as easy to ignore Christopher. On the school bus I always sat next to Jaime Mitchell, my best friend who lived down the road from us. She'd save me a seat so I wouldn't have to sit next to him, and he'd sit up in front with the little kids. But then he'd start doing something like humming out loud to himself—like for a while he was stuck on humming the "Barney and Friends" song, which when he did the kids would start telling him to shut up, but then he'd just cover his ears and say, "I can't hear you! I can't hear you! I can't hear you!" over and over, until he ran out of breath or passed out, which he actually did one time. The driver stopped the bus and everything and made me go up there and take care of him. How mortifying.

Another thing he did because of Barney was run around randomly hugging people, whether they wanted a hug or not. No one within arm's length was safe. Ms. Beetle, his special ed teacher at the time, she tried to get him to stop, but Mom and Aunt Carrie and most other adults thought it was cute, which only made him do it more. It sure wasn't cute to the kids at school; sometimes they would shove him away and call him names or swear at him, and it wasn't cute to strangers in public.

One time our family was on vacation in Washington, D.C., and we were taking a tour of the Capitol building, and right in the hallway outside of Senate chamber—you know, where you go through the metal detectors before going into the visitors' gallery?— Christopher got bored waiting and decided to start hugging everyone in our tour group. So this important-looking old guy in a suit came up to our group and was standing by the lady giving the tour, looking all friendly, when Christopher came along going, "And I love you, too," while he put his arms around the man and started squeezing the smile out of him. The security guards were over there in a New York second pulling Christopher off this man, who it turns out was *Senator Ted Kennedy!* I could have just died. Instead I tried blending in with this family from Japan.

I spent a lot of time trying to escape from Christopher—partly because Mom and Dad made me take care of him so much, and also because at school I was embarrassed to be seen around him. It wasn't just that he always acted like a kid half his age. That might've been cute, like the mentally handicapped kids they show on TV. But he isn't cute like that. Okay, I know that sounds mean, but it's true—he's all crooked. He's got crooked teeth inside a crooked mouth. He used to walk crooked because of his special shoes. His face is really long, like it was made out of pulled taffy or something, and his big ears stick out. And he talks in a low, slurred voice, like his tongue is swollen or something. Also he gets spit on you when he gets excited and starts stuttering.

I'm not saying he couldn't be cute at all; he had a funny smile, so whenever he started laughing, you couldn't keep from laughing, too. He was always doing things to make me and Mom and Dad laugh. We'd always say, "Silly old bear!" whenever he did something totally off the wall. But at school I guess I was afraid that people wouldn't like me as much if I hung around Christopher, because most of the kids avoided him.

Around that time we were studying genetics in science class—you know, Gregor Mendel, that monk who discovered heredity in petunias or peas or something. I'd always sort of wondered why Christopher was mentally handicapped and I wasn't. I would lie in bed at night listening to Christopher sleep in his room across the hall and think about that.

Well, I found out when we studied Mendel that it's more or less chance: how your parents' genes get combined decides whether you're tall or short, have blond or brown hair, or whether you're mentally handicapped or not. It was like a light going on over my head: Whatever happened to make Christopher the way he was could have just as easily happened to me. It was just chance. Just luck. Or bad luck, if you were Christopher.

For a while I even worried that what the kids said about "retard germs" was partly true—that maybe I had some of the genes that Christopher had. I would look in the mirror to check that my ears didn't stick out, and I got totally obsessed with doing good on tests and homework to prove that I wasn't dumb like him. For a while I even got straight A's.

Mom told me I didn't have to worry about it. She said, "Even if you did have the same genes as Christopher, we would still love you, just like we love your brother," which is what I figured she would say, so it didn't make me feel too much better.

In high school I did pretty good in classes and I got on the track team and I landed a part in a couple plays. I stopped worrying so much about myself, and I started thinking more about what life was like for Christopher. I was leaving him behind more and more often; then I got my driver's license and started dating and looking at colleges, too. Christopher missed the boat on all those things; he was always a few steps behind the rest of the band.

And people are mean to him for it. The kids at school were always picking on him as much as they could get away with, especially guys like Mac Towley, Corey Flint, and Greg Puerilmen. Christopher made it easy for them, too, by trying to make friends with them, probably because they were the only ones paying attention to him. They'd play him like a puppet on a string: Christopher would give them his lunch money if they asked, and then sit with them in the cafeteria watching them eat his food, hoping for the leftovers. Or they would tell him to do things that would get him in trouble, and he'd go do them.

Like this one time those guys convinced him that he should bring flowers to Ms. Kendall, the high school special education teacher. It was so obvious that he had a crush on her, because like everything else, he didn't even bother to hide it. He was always looking at her all starry-eyed, which everyone thought was really funny, since it made Ms. Kendall squirm. So they gave Christopher a pair of scissors and told him to go over to this house across the street from the school and cut some zinnias and marigolds and snapdragons and things from the garden. I don't know whether they told him the guy wouldn't mind or what, but Christopher went over there and cut a ton of flowers. I can just imagine him grinning and talking to himself and happily snipping away.

The old man who planted the flowers was so furious he called the police. Of course, Ms. Kendall figured out where he had gotten the flowers, and the school liaison officer ended up having a little chat with Christopher. And I got called down to the office because the secretary couldn't get a hold of Mom or Dad.

The secretary's like, "Well, your brother ruined this guy's garden, and he wants someone to pay for it." And I'm going, okay, so what am I supposed to do about it? Am I my brother's baby-sitter? But of course I didn't say anything except that I would tell my parents.

As I left the office, I passed by where the liaison officer was talking with Christopher.

I have this picture in my mind of the officer crouched down in front of Christopher, who's bawling his eyes out because he's scared of the police. The kids going by were staring, and Christopher still had a bunch of those stupid flowers in his hand, even though they were all broken and hanging down. And then I turned away because I couldn't stand to watch it anymore.

Jaime had started driving her parents' second car to school, this old Buick, and me and Megan Chantely were getting rides to school from her so we didn't have to take the bus. I didn't really like Megan that much, because of how stuck-up she was. When her family moved here from New York, they bought a house in Gardenia Heights, the newest development outside of town, and she acted like she was a big fish in a small pond. She was more Jaime's friend than mine, but I put up with her because Jaime did.

So we're driving along eating those little Tic Tac candies and talking about, you know, normal stuff—like who's going to prom with who, and this guy Brian I had a crush on—when all of a sudden Megan goes, "So, Lily, what was up with your brother? Why was he crying?"

"He got in trouble," I said.

"For what?"

"I guess he took some flowers out of some guy's yard."

"Why'd he do that?"

"How am I supposed to know?" I snapped.

Nobody said anything for a moment. She was making me mad, and she knew it, too. Then she said, "Is it because he's retarded?"

"Mentally handicapped," I said.

She leans over the backseat and goes, "Maybe your parents should send him to one of those institutions where he wouldn't get into trouble."

I turned around and glared at her. "What a stupid thing to say!"

She's looking all surprised and hurt, like she's clueless about why I'm getting mad. "What? Don't you think it would be better for everyone? He would be happier, and he wouldn't be as much trouble to everyone else."

"They should put people like *you* in institutions," I said.

"Excuse me?" Fortunately, Jaime pulled up in front of Megan's house just then. "You don't have to bite my head off," Megan said. "I was just trying to be helpful."

"Mind your own business, Megan," I said.

Jaime was looking back and forth between us. Megan got out of the car, glaring at me the whole time. "Some people are *so* sensitive," she said, and then she slammed the door.

I just kept biting my lip and wanting to cry. Jaime started driving again, but she didn't know what to say. After a while she goes, "Megan's so shallow, she wouldn't get your ankles wet."

I looked over at her, and Jaime looked back at me, and then we both started laughing our heads off. I was laughing so hard I accidentally snorted up the Tic Tac in my mouth, and then I sneezed and it came flying out my nose. That made us laugh even harder, so Jaime had to pull over to the side of the road. After about five minutes she wiped her eyes and then reached over and hugged me.

"Oh, now I have to pee," I said, and that got us laughing all over again.

When I got home I went up to Christopher's room and knocked on the door. He was lying on his bed, curled up like a baby, chewing on his thumb. I sat down on the bed beside him. Didn't touch him or anything; just sat there looking at him.

"'Topher," I said, "I told you not to hang around those guys. They don't want to be your friend. They're just mean. So don't listen to what they say, okay? Don't be a silly old bear."

But he didn't say anything, just moved his head to look out the window. He could get like that sometimes, real quiet. You'd wonder what he was thinking about, if he thought about anything at all.

Later that night I told Mom and Dad that the guys at school had gotten Christopher in trouble again. They said they would call Mr. Benning, the principal, again—not that it ever did any good.

"We can't protect Christopher from everything," Dad said. "Some of life's lessons he's going to have to learn himself, the hard way."

"Why did God make Christopher the way he is?" I asked.

Mom was doing dishes at the sink, and she smiled faintly. "Sometimes we wonder the same thing. We asked that same question a lot after Christopher was born. And you know what?" She paused like she was wondering whether she should tell me. "I think the answer God gave us is that Christopher is like a box that comes in the mail wrapped in plain old brown shipping paper. It takes a long time to unwrap, but if you're patient enough, you'll find something good inside. A gift from God."

I was thinking about him lying in his bed upstairs, silently hurting. "Yeah, well," I said, "I don't think it's fair—to Christopher, I mean. I wouldn't want to be in his shoes. Is the gift really worth it all?"

"Is it?" Mom asked, raising her eyebrows. "What do you think?"

I didn't know the answer to that question until I went away for my freshman year at college. I missed Christopher, and I wondered why. And then I realized I missed him because I loved him, and that surprised me. Maybe it took this distance between us for me to be able to figure that out—you know how they say you don't know what you've got 'til it's gone?

It makes me think about the time Christopher taught me how to wake up bees.

This happened very early one summer morning. I was going out to clean my horse's stall, and I saw Christopher out by the flowers that Mom planted along the side-yard fence. He was leaning over them, real still. That got my curiosity up, since if Christopher's not making noise, he's usually getting in trouble, so I went over there. "What're you doing, 'Topher?"

He starts shushing me and says, "Be very, very quiet," which almost made me laugh because he sounded like Elmer Fudd. Then I saw he had his nose right over a big, fat bumblebee that was curled up in the center of one of the cosmos, with the soft pink petals fanned out around it like a teacup.

I thought the bee was dead, but Christopher tipped it out of the flower and into the palm of his hand. He held it up close to his mouth and gently blew warm breath onto it.

The bee's little wings began fluttering. They looked like glass.

"Careful, Christopher, it'll sting you," I said, but he just shook his head. And then all of a sudden it just flew away. We watched it until it was just a bright speck in the sunlight.

I was astonished. "How do you like that?" I said.

Christopher grins at me and goes, "I like it."

I don't know where he learned that. He still goes out into the garden early on summer mornings, when the dew is still on the flowers, and finds the bees that hid there overnight so he can wake them up.

I know it sounds cheesy, but I guess maybe Christopher is sort of like those bees—I was afraid if I got too close, I'd get stung. And I just might get stung, too. Like I'm starting to think about the fact that when Mom and Dad are gone, I'll have to watch out for him, and that won't be easy.

But I think it'll be worth it. Besides, the thing with the bees got me curious about what other tricks this boy might know.

The First Sorrowful Mystery

They whipped young Moses for stealing collard greens. His father, Gabriel, had known in his heart that there would be trouble with Moses, who harbored the same slow-burning anger at the Colonel and the overseer that Gabriel himself had felt when he was younger and stronger. Moses was as big as any man on the plantation, too, and as a result, fearless. "If the devil shook a stick at him, he'd hit the devil right back," Sally, the cook who worked for Old Mistress in the big house, would say.

Moses had taken the collard greens from Old Mistress's garden, and cooked them up with the rest of supper. Everyone sitting around the fire knew they were stolen. Someone had called out to him, "Hey, Moses, where'd you get them fine collard greens?" and Moses had grinned and replied, "Why, I 'spect they just growed here," and everyone laughed. Folks swiped things here and there all the time; mostly the Colonel didn't bother about it. But the Mistress had been meaning to have collard greens that Sunday for supper, and when she found them missing, she sent the Colonel to find out who took them.

The Colonel was a handsome man with a military bearing: sharp-faced, neatly groomed, and known throughout the county as an excellent horseman and a good Christian. When he came to the slaves' cook fire asking about the missing greens, Moses immediately confessed to stealing them. The Colonel commenced to give Moses a long lecture on the sinfulness of stealing, beginning with, "You should know better, your pappy being a preacher and all," and ending with, "Now promise me you won't do it again," with lots of quotes from the Bible in between.

"But Massa," Moses replied innocently, "The Bible says I didn't steal them collard greens."

"Tell me where in the Bible it says so," the Colonel said coolly.

"'You shall reap what you sow,' and that's the Gospel truth. I done sowed them collard greens, and I done reaped them."

Gabriel, who was among those looking on, got a prickly feeling all over. Moses may as well have been throwing rocks at a rattler, the way he was acting so uppity with the Colonel, who had turned red in the face. The Colonel was the sort of man who got quieter as he got angrier, and now he didn't say a word. He turned on the heel of his boot and marched off toward the house.

Gabriel went to Moses and grabbed him by the arm. He had to look up at his son to talk to him. "Why'd you say a fool thing like that?" he asked.

"Because it's the truth," Moses said, watching after the Colonel. "It ain't right that I work all day an' don't have nothing to show for it but what he chooses to throw to me, like a dog under the table."

"You could'a told him you wouldn't steal no more," Gabriel said. "What you want to be whupped for? You think you stronger than the whip?"

"Maybe."

The Colonel returned with his son Joe, and the overseer, Will Brady, who carried a gun. The Colonel carried the bullwhip. They tied Moses' hands to a rope, and the rope to an old pine tree in the yard, so that he could barely touch the ground with his toes.

The Colonel whipped him good. It was quiet, except for the lazy buzz of flies and the lonely call of some bird out in the woods, and in the silence the whip sang all the louder, as if it were alive. It hissed through the air like cold water on a hot iron, and it cracked down with a sound like breaking kindling. Some folks watching cried. Gabriel did not, because he had seen his wife die in childbirth and all his seven children except Moses sold away from him. He'd given up crying long ago.

For some time—ten minutes, perhaps—Moses did not cry out, either. He was too proud and angry and stubborn. But by and by, when all of his back glistened red, and the blood soaked the ground darkly, and his whole body trembled, then finally he called out in a hoarse whisper: "Massa, do pray! Do pray, Massa."

The Colonel relented then, taking off his hat and wiping the sweat from his brow. After a moment, he called to Joe to bring him the salt, which he then poured onto Moses' raw back, to make it burn and come up blisters. Moses writhed on the end of the rope like a half-dead fish on a line, his mouth slack as he moaned from the pain. Gabriel noticed that even Joe—good old Joe, who had grown up with Moses, even gone coon hunting with him last summer—turned away and held his hands tightly behind his back.

And then the overseer cut Moses down from the rope and left him lying there in the bloody dirt.

Gabriel, with help from George and Sally, managed to carry him into the cabin, where they washed the blood and salt off him as best they could. Sally wrapped his back in sheets smeared with grease, to keep them from sticking to his back when the blood dried. She murmured softly to Moses the whole time.

But she said nothing to Gabriel, which he took as a way of saying, "I told you so." It was the unspoken opinion of Sally and many others that he should have let Moses run off to freedom when the boy had wanted to a few months back. A boy like that was spoiling for trouble; better to let him join up with the Federals and find it in the war than find it with the Colonel, where he had no chance at all. But Gabriel had advised Moses against running off.

He told him about the slave hounds: "Them hounds! They's tore apart plenty a man. My mammy done run away once. Them dogs went right straight to the ditch where she was hid, and they tore most of her clothes off and bit her all over. When they brought her in, she was a sight to see—all covered with blood and dirt. No sir, you don't want to fool with them dogs."

Moses would not be scared off by hounds, though. "I'll fool them hounds," he'd say. "I'll walk along the top of a fence, or down the middle of the river a ways." Then Gabriel said things such as, "No use runnin' from bad to worse, lookin' for better," and, "Every man has to serve God under his own vine and fig tree." Moses never did run off, but only because he loved his father and wouldn't stand against him. But even love of his father couldn't make his spirit bend to the will of the overseer or the Colonel.

Gabriel wanted to explain to Sally and the others that he had only been protecting Moses from the hounds, or from getting hung. Or sold, like so much livestock. They probably believed he had kept Moses with him out of selfishness. Well, and wasn't it natural for a man to expect his only remaining son to stay with him and be a comfort to him in his old age? Didn't the Bible say, "Honor thy father and mother"?

For the next two days, Sally ministered to Moses with ointments, cool rags, and whiskey. Gabriel sat there with him and brushed away the blood-hungry flies, feeling guiltier and guiltier all the time. Nine plagues had been visited on Pharaoh when he didn't let Moses of the Old Testament go, Gabriel thought, nine plagues and the death of all the firstborn sons.

"Is he gonna die?" Gabriel asked Sally.

She gave him a long look of pity. "No, I don't 'spect the Lord will take him jus' yet, Gabe," she said softly.

On the third night after the whipping, Gabriel had a dream. He dreamed that all the people sneaked off to a brush arbor in the woods, the way they did every Sunday night, for their own secret prayer meeting. Down by the river, they would sing praises as they pleased, and God would meet them there. Gabriel cut a fine figure as a preacher, with his snow-white beard and Gospel voice. And because he could read, he would preach from the parts of the Bible the white preachers tended to forget when addressing slaves, which was most parts.

In his dream Gabriel was baptizing people in the dark, star-speckled river, and preaching in this way: "The Lord says, 'Love your enemies, do good to those who hate you! Bless those who curse you! Pray for those what beat you and whip you! Love your enemy, and you'll get back good measure pressed down, shaken t'gether and runnin' over!'"

And the people assembled there shouted, "Amen, amen!"

"Love your enemy! Do good to those who hate you!" Gabriel called out.

"Amen!"

"Pray for those who beat you!"

"Amen, amen!" the people chanted.

"Look!" he shouted, like a man gone crazy. "Look upon the cross, the sign of our salvation!" and then there was Moses, hanging from the pine tree, the blood pouring out of him, looking at Gabriel with eyes that were as dark and deep as the river itself.

It was such an awful sight, he woke up crying and shouting. A hand clamped over his mouth, and another held down his arm when he started to strike out, and for a moment it was as if he were still dreaming; he thought perhaps he was wrestling an angel, as Jacob had, but it was only Moses' face that breathed on his, whispering, "Hush! Hush now!"

"You's alive!" Gabriel exclaimed.

"'Course I's alive!" Moses said. "Ol' Massa pretty near killed me, but not quite. I sure is in a fix, though. Hurts somethin' awful every time I move."

The cabin was mostly dark, although the moon cast an oblong patch of light through the window. Gabriel ran his hand over Moses' face, feeling the contours of his jaw, his mouth, his eyes. "What you doin' awake now, chile? You want more whiskey?"

Moses was leaning heavily against the bunk. "No, I was only thirsty," he said. "Pappy, I been thinking."

"Thinking on what?"

"I been thinking—I is gonna run away to a free state. I ain't gonna put up with this treatment any longer. I can't stand much more."

Gabriel winced inwardly. "Well, you ain't gonna run away tonight."

"Oh, Pappy," Moses said lowly, looking away. "I sure is."

"What? You don't know what you talkin' 'bout, boy!"

"Shh! You want to wake up everyone?"

"How are you going to run away like that? You can barely stand up straight! And you's so full of blood, you may as well tie a ham to your bottom for the hounds to follow!"

Moses was silent for a minute. "That may be so," he said quietly, "but now's the best time to go. Ol' Massa won't be lookin' for me in the field yet, after he beat me so bad. Now, listen here: When you go out to the fields, if you-all says I's still all laid up gettin' over that whuppin', he's gonna believe you. That be good for a day's start, maybe more."

"He'll kill you," Gabriel said. "Can you get that through your head? He'll kill you!"

"If he can catch me," Moses said. "And if he does—better to die free than die a slave. You say, 'Don't go runnin' from bad to worse, lookin' for better.' Well, worse done come lookin' for me, and it ain't gonna get no better, neither."

Gabriel knew the boy was right, but it was hard to admit, because it would mean letting him go—and to a place where Gabriel would have no power to protect him. It was foolish to imagine that he could keep Moses safe at all—the scars on the boy's back were testament to that—but the dangers here were familiar, at least.

He turned away and shut his eyes. Half-asleep yet, he was still haunted by the dream. It was blasphemy to dream of his own son hanging there like Jesus on the cross, unless it was a sign. That would be just like God, always sending you a sign or speaking in parables, then leaving you to figure out the meaning.

Gabriel saw the dream face of Moses again, those eyes like a question, and suddenly it came to him clearly: God wanted Moses for himself. God wanted him to give up Moses the same way God wanted Abraham to sacrifice Isaac, the same way God had sent his own Son to be crucified. God wanted Moses for himself, and was asking Gabriel to hand him over.

It made Gabriel shudder to think of God's hunger.

After a moment, he turned to Moses, who was waiting. "I prayed to God 'bout what to do," he said, placing a hand on the boy's head, partly in blessing and partly in remembrance of when Moses was small. "God says, 'Let Moses go.'" He smiled, faintly. "An' I ain't so foolish as to go against the will of God. So I's lettin' you go. God watch over you."

"God will," Moses said. Gabriel smiled again, knowing such confidence came not from an unwavering faith but from ignorance. God watched over Jesus, too, and Jesus got crucified.

Moses left that same night, in the third hour before dawn, with a forged pass that Gabriel wrote, and grease smeared on the bottom of his feet, to throw the dogs off his scent.

But as luck would have it, early the next morning the Colonel came to check on Moses ("Ol' Massa sure is concerned about his health now, ain't he?" George commented). When the Colonel found him gone, he sent for the patrollers who kept the slave hounds, and his son Joe.

"Now look here," the Colonel told Joe, "you're almost a grown man, and it's time you started taking a man's responsibility. I can't afford to lose that young buck—he's worth fifteen hundred dollars, at least. And if he gets away, every man, woman, and child on the place is going to try the same thing. I'd go after him myself, but I got business here to attend to. You go with Will here, and the patrollers. You go and tree that ol' coon and bring him back here. I'll give him such a whippin', the next time he decides to run off, he'll have to do it crawlin'."

"Yessir," Joe said, mounting his horse. The patrollers, a lean-looking lot of men, had come with the hounds, which were baying and straining at their leashes. Joe glanced at Gabriel, who took a step forward, silently pleading, but then the boy ducked under the brim of his slouch hat. His face looked ashen.

Gabriel prayed all that day as he worked in the fields, hoeing between rows of cotton. He talked to the Lord, muttering under his breath: "O Lord, I's only tryin' to do your will, Lord, an' you know how hard a time I have figurin' out jus' what that is, sometimes, Lord, 'cause I's jus' a stupid man. So if it ain't your will, Lord, for Moses to run away to freedom, then I sure is sorry for that; only have mercy on us, Lord, 'cause I'm down here all alone, an' it would sure break my heart to lose that boy, it sure would."

He went on like that all day, pounding at the dirt angrily with the hoe, and praying, because it was all he could do.

Joe returned shortly before dusk, as the sun was falling bright-red out of the sky. Folks drifted out of their cabins; even Old Mistress stepped out onto the porch of the big house. Will Brady was with him, and the patrollers, who hung back a ways. The hounds looked beat. Gabriel walked forward and stood under the whipping tree, watching Joe dismount from his horse.

The Colonel came across the yard. "Well, where is he?" he called.

Joe looked down at his muddy boots. He carried a shotgun at his side, and his pants were all bloody. He looked up at his father.

"I done killed him."

Gabriel cried out and lurched forward, as if he would grab at Joe; but a glance from the Colonel stopped him, and he halted in mid-stride, stricken, his face twisted and his hands fists that seemed poised to beat at the air.

"What did you do a blame-fool thing like that for?" the Colonel demanded.

The boy shrugged. "I ambushed him, hiding in the brush. He put up a fight, so I shot him. Was him or me. I figured you'd rather have me alive than him."

The Colonel turned to the overseer. "Will, is that so?"

The overseer bowed his head and coughed some. "I'm right sorry, sir, but we split up, so we were pretty far away from Joe. We didn't know he'd found the boy 'til we heard the shots, and then we came as quick as we could. But by then the nigger was dead, of course."

"Where's the body?"

"Left it there," the overseer said shortly, as if this were the obvious thing to do. "We didn't carry a shovel with us, an' it was getting too near dark to fool with makin' a drag sledge."

The Colonel glowered darkly, and everything was silent, except for the flies. Finally he said, "Well, ain't no use cryin' over spilt milk. You niggers! What are you standin' around here for? Yes, you ought to cry; it's all the more work for you. Now let this be a lesson to you, not to run off. Joe, put up that horse, an' come to the house."

And then the Colonel ambled off to where Mistress was standing on the porch, her hands on her hips. Gabriel could hear him telling her: "He shot him dead! Can you believe that?"

George and Charlie came over to Gabriel, and Charlie put his hand on his shoulder. "Let me be," Gabriel said, shrugging it off. He walked toward where Joe was putting his horse up in the barn.

He was not thinking of how God had let him down; he was not thinking at all. The grief in his heart was pure white, and it tasted like metal in his mouth. The barn door opened onto the blackness inside, and he entered into it, breathing in the strong scent of hay and manure and animal flesh. He paused inside to let his eyes adjust. Joe was with his horse at the far end of the barn. There was a pitchfork nearby, and Gabriel took that in his hands.

A voice seemed to whisper to him: "Love your enemy! Do good to those who hate you!"

He ignored it, and walked on.

"God loved you so, he gave up his only son," the voice said.

The boy was a fool not to hear him coming, not to turn around to light a lantern to see by. Live by the sword, die by the sword, Gabriel thought.

"Take up your cross and follow me!" the voice persisted.

No, Gabriel answered. I've had about all I can take of crosses and crucifixions and whippings and what not. There won't be no more if I can help it. Turn around, boy.

He was standing three paces behind Joe, who was currying the horse with a brush, stroking it and speaking to it in soft tones. Gabriel raised the pitchfork up, holding it like a lance. Turn around, boy.

Joe turned, and Gabriel saw his face, and Gabriel recognized it as the boyish face of his dead son's childhood friend. Something awful seized Gabriel—something like love for that boy, and it was awful because the boy had killed his son. It surprised him like a punch in the face. He let the pitchfork drop, stumbled away backward and fell down.

"Gabe!" Joe said, crouching beside him. "Don't worry, Gabe—I won't hurt you." He was gripping the old man's arm so hard,

Gabriel didn't believe him. "Moses ain't dead, Gabe!"

Gabriel gaped at him. "His blood is all over you!"

"No—it's just the blood of a boar we killed," Joe said quickly; he was excited. "Be still a minute; I'll tell you what happened, quick before my pa comes. I tracked Moses down, the way I did when we was little an' playin' in the woods. I said, 'Hey, Moses,' and he said hey back, and we argued some about whether I would bring him back here, which I was inclined to do since lettin' him free would be about the same as stealin', I figured. But then this boar came trottin' down the trail, and Moses said, 'See, there's a sign to you to let me go.'" He paused, thoughtful.

"You ever see a boar come trottin' straight at you careless as a gentleman in the park on a Sunday afternoon?" he asked. Gabriel shook his head mutely. "No, I never seen such a thing neither. So I shot that boar, easy as pickin' ripe apples off a tree, and I sprinkled the blood all over Moses, to make like it was him what was shot. When ol' Will Brady an' them other scoundrels showed up with the hounds on account of hearing my gun, I made all weepy-like, pretendin' I was mournful that I'd shot Moses. I sure was scared they'd shoot him again for good luck or kick him or some such, but they believed it. Wasn't that a good plan, Gabe? Wasn't that fine? Moses thought it up, too." He inclined his head to one side, as if listening for something outside. "I couldn't kill Moses. I don't know. I ain't sure I done the right thing lettin' him go, but I couldn't kill him, and bringin' him back here might've been the same thing. Now, you better make all mournful yourself for a while. Don't you walk out this barn grinnin'."

"Moses—ain't dead?" Gabe whispered hoarsely.

"No," Joe said, "he ain't."

And because Gabriel believed him, he cried.

Choosing Sides

The problem with the Flanders boy began when his family moved into the white house next door, which had been empty for more than a year. This was during Christmas break, so Alex Shepherdson, who lived in the brick bungalow next door, was on hand to watch them move in. Alex's Starter jacket was zipped up tight, and his dark blue scarf had been wrapped tightly around his neck by his mother. He stood out in the front yard, behind the low wall of one of the neighborhood's many snow forts, and stared.

There were children in the new family: a boy who seemed to be about his age and a girl who was a bit younger. They were noisy, and went everywhere at a dead run with their coats flapping open and their knit hats bobbing. They explored the yard and the inside of the house and shouted questions to the father and mother, who brought small boxes from the moving van into the house while shouting back at the children. The father, a squat, muscular man with thinning blond hair and a mustache, divided his attention between yelling at the children and the moving men, who never said a word as far as Alex could tell.

The boy and the girl eventually found their way around the hedge that separated the two yards and came up short when they found Alex staring at them. "Hi," the boy said, raising a soggy mitten in greeting the way Indians did on television. "My name's Zack Flanders, and this is Patience." The girl wiped her runny nose with the back of her hand. Both of them had wild red hair and freckles and large teeth.

"My name's Alex," Alex said. "Where are you from?"

"Well, we've lived all over the place," Zack said loudly. "But mostly we're from Canada. That's where me and my sister were born. That's where my gramma lives still. We're not going to get to visit her anymore, though, because it's too far, and besides, she's in a nursing home."

"I never knew any foreigners before," Alex said.

"Do you live here?" Zack asked.

Alex nodded and added that he had a brother named Grant.

"You can be our friend," Zack said. He turned to Patience and, as if she hadn't heard him the first time, explained, "He's going to be our friend."

Alex worried a little about that—who knew if they would be friends or not?—but before he knew it, Zack was over the wall and in his fort, and Patience was following clumsily behind. Zack looked at the wall of packed snow, which curved around in a half circle against the higher range of snow hills pushed up from the street by the plow. He noticed a cave scooped out of one of the mounds. An old yellow towel hung frozen solid from a stick stuck in the highest hill. The fort formed a defense against a similar structure on the other side of the street, where the Martinez boys lived.

"Cool!" Zack said. He scrambled up the snow to the flag, which he grabbed hold of and began waving wildly, shouting, "I'm king of the hill! King of the hill!"

"You're not supposed to stand up there," Alex called. "You'll wreck it!" He meant the cave underneath would collapse.

Patience smiled wickedly and ran after her brother. "No you're not!" she shrieked.

"Yes I am," Zack taunted. "I'm king of the hill, and you can't get me!"

Patience made her way up the snow hill. The boy allowed her to get to the top and then gave her an effortless shove that sent her tumbling backward down the hill. She jumped to her feet again and made another assault. Chunks of snow were falling off the hill.

"Get off! You're wrecking it!" Alex repeated. He was getting mad; he had worked on this fort for hours, and once it was ruined it would be hard to rebuild.

"I'll bet you can't get me off here," Zack said. Before Alex could even try, however, Mr. Flanders came over to the hedge and started yelling at his kids to get their butts over there right now before he came and got them. The kids obeyed immediately, shoving each other as they went.

"I'll see you later," Zack said, punching Alex in the arm in a way that meant to be friendly but actually hurt. "See you tomorow," Patience yelled, turning around and wiping her nose at the same time.

I don't think I like that kid, Alex thought.

His parents seemed to like the new neighbors plenty well.

"Maybe they'll keep up the lawn better than the realtor did," their father said at supper. The weeds in that yard got two feet tall last summer.

No one needed to be reminded of that, because Mr. Shepherdson had complained about the weeds all summer long.

"I don't think so," Alex said. "They look like dorks." His mother gave him a sharp look.

"I told you I don't want to hear you calling people names," she said.

"But they are, Mom," Alex said. "They came over and started fooling around in our fort, and they were wrecking it and stuff, and they wouldn't stop."

"Oh, wah, wah, they're ruining my fort!" Alex's brother, Grant, who was fourteen, mimicked. "Don't be such a baby."

Alex tried kicking him under the table but missed.

"You boys wreck each other's forts all the time anyway," their father said.

"That's different," Alex said, talking through a mouthful of mashed potatoes. "That's only when we're playing war."

"You boys should make friends with those new kids," their mother said. "It's hard moving to a new school in the middle of the year. Think of what it would be like for you to be in their shoes."

"They're not even my age," Grant said. "Alex can make friends with them."

"I'll be friends with them if they'll be friendly," Alex said sourly.

Actually, the problem was that they were too friendly, in a rude way. For instance, the next day the new boy followed Alex and Micah Miljah inside the house without being invited. Alex had brought Micah over to play Nintendo. Zack had been out in his front yard with his sister, who was sitting in the snow crying very loudly. Neither of them had mittens or coats on.

Zack simply followed the two boys into the Shepherdson home, and Alex didn't realize it until the new boy was in the door. He turned around and said sharply: "Hey! This isn't your house!" And then he started pushing Zack out.

But then his mother intervened. She invited Zack inside and offered him hot chocolate besides. Then she pulled Alex aside to chew him out for not being friendlier. So for the next two hours he and Micah were forced to play with Zack. They made sure he didn't hog the game, though.

Zack started coming over every day for hours at a time, even staying for supper. He didn't seem to notice Alex ignoring him or being rude to him (as rude as he could be around his mother). No matter what Alex did, Zack hung around like a stray dog that won't stop following you but keeps slobbering all over your shoes and tripping over your heels.

Things came to a head one evening when the whole neighborhood was out at the same time and got together a friendly game of war. Joey and Tom Macalaster from down the street came over, and so did Carrie Glendening (who was a girl but had a boy's throwing arm), and Micah Miljah, and hound-faced Peter Dostov, and of course the Martinez twins.

Even Grant, who usually had better things to
do, joined up on Alex's side.

They divided into two teams and set up
operations on opposite sides of the street,
building defenses and hard-packed snowball ammunition behind the range of snow
mounds. The street was the demilitarized
zone, which forces from either side crossed
at the risk of being pulverized by a barrage
of snowballs. The object was to capture the
other side's flag without getting captured and
held prisoner.

They worked excitedly, happily consulting
one another and scheming and engineering.
Their cheeks were numbed and reddened by
the sharp cold, which also made their breath
come out in large white clouds. The yellow
light of the streetlamp cast otherworldly
shadows, and steam rose from the manhole
covers in the street. The heavy boots and
coats they wore seemed soldierly. They felt
as if they were truly going off to war.

Soon they began the fighting, and the air
above the road filled with white arcing mis-
siles. When everyone's arms got tired, and
things let up a bit, Grant called Alex, Micah,
and Carrie—who were all on the same
side—to the snow cave to plan strategy.
Grant played football in school, and was
fond of strategy. He described how several
of them would keep up some good forward

fire while he and Micah did an end-run, slipping up unnoticed behind the other side
from the end of the block.

As they were crouched there whispering
in the snow, the boy Zack came running up
behind them, yelling a war whoop at the top
of his lungs. He hurled himself in among
them, hitting Grant and Carrie squarely.

"I got you! You're my prisoners now," he
boasted, grinning.

"What're you doing?" Grant demanded,
shoving him away.

"You're supposed to attack them, not us!"
Carrie said. "You've got to follow the rules if
you're going to play."

Zack sat up, panting happily, hatless and
bright-eyed. He didn't say anything, only
clambered up the hill above the snow cave.
A flurry of snowballs sent him stumbling
back. "Come on, you guys! Let's get 'em!" he
shouted.

"We're planning strategy," Alex explained.

"Who needs strategy?" Zack said. "We'll
squash them like bugs!" Grant looked at
Micah and shook his head.

"We're outnumbered anyway," Micah pointed out. "He would be a good distraction."

So Micah and Grant went crawling
through the snow down several houses to
where the street was darkest, then made a
dash across. Alex and Carrie threw snowballs

as fast as they could from low behind their snow pile, but Zack worked from atop it, yelling all the time. Finally a snowball exploded in his face, and he fell over backward into the trench where Alex and Carrie were.

"I've been hit," he croaked melodramatically.

"I hope you die," Carrie said, and Alex laughed. But then he felt guilty, and before he knew it he was saying, "Here, you can make snowballs for us for a while." He thought about how his better nature came out at the worst times.

But instead of being grateful, Zack sat up and said, "I don't want to make snowballs. My hands are cold."

"Well, then don't make snowballs," Alex said irritably.

There was a ruckus on the other side of the street that was Grant and Micah getting pounded by the enemy. Alex, Carrie, and Zack poked their heads up to see what was going on, but could only make out legs and arms flailing above the snow. By the sound of the other side's cheering, it seemed that the mission had been a complete failure.

Peter Dostov made an appearance to announce that they'd taken Micah and Grant prisoner. Alex and Carrie groaned.

"We're doomed," Alex said.

"No we're not!" Zack said. "Wait here." And he went running off to his house, his coat flying like a cape behind him.

"As if we're going anywhere," Carrie said snottily.

The silver lining in the situation was that the other side had to guard the prisoners, which meant Alex and Carrie weren't nearly as outnumbered as they would have been otherwise. Still, there was no doubt that they were fighting a losing battle. The other side even started making daring sorties directly across the street toward their flag.

Just as things looked bleakest—three of the other boys coming at them at once— Zack showed up, looking like a hero. Alex wondered what he was up to until he pulled out the Super Soaker water gun and began giving the other side a good water-ing down, making them retreat almost immediately with angry howls—which Zack ignored. In fact, he kept pumping a steady stream of water at them. He got the two guards—Tom Macalaster and Tony Martinez—full in the face, and when Grant and Micah stood up to see what was going on, he got them, too.

Alex and Carrie were up on their hill now, yelling at Zack to stop, stop—because he was ruining everything again—but he was up on the enemy's hill, grabbing the flag and making a run for it. He returned with the flag raised over his head triumphantly, smiling and whooping.

"You stupid idiot!" Alex yelled at him.

The others gathered around Zack like mean dogs. The water stains on their coats, hats, and pants—he'd gotten one of them in an embarrassing place—were beginning to stiffen and freeze, making crinkly noises as they approached.

"What are you doing?" Grant said furiously. "Give me that!" He reached out to take the Super Soaker.

Zack looked worried for the first time since Alex had known him. He backed away, then actually turned and ran toward his house. The boys who had gotten wet paused just a second before chasing him. Zack fled into his house and slammed the door, and they stood around in the yard yelling threats after him until his mother came out.

"He sprayed us with water," one of the boys said.

"I don't care what he did!" the mother responded fiercely. Her hair was all tangled, and her neck looked ropy.

"Get out of my yard!" she yelled.

Everyone moved out of the yard in an angry mood. They hung around for a while lamely fantasizing about how they would get back at Zack, but the discussion ended quickly because most of them were getting cold from being wet.

"The little twerp better watch his step," Grant muttered darkly as they went inside. Alex felt good now that the whole neighborhood saw what a pain Zack was. Maybe the kid would leave him alone.

Actually, just the opposite happened. Alex was in his bedroom stripping off his soggy clothes so he could take a hot bath when he heard a strange howling that began low in pitch and climbed higher and higher into a screech that broke into short yelps that sounded like some awful beast dying somewhere dark. A chill raised the skin all over Alex's body.

He stood perfectly still for a long moment. He could hear the evening news on the television in the den, distantly. The unearthly howling noise was coming from outside. He crept up to his window and pushed the shade aside slightly and peered out.

Illuminated by the porch light in the backyard of the Flanders house was a picture of violence that Alex had never witnessed before: the Flanders boy, held roughly by the arm, being kicked by his father again and again in the butt and the legs and the stomach. It was Zack who was making that awful noise, and now Alex could hear under it the father's growly voice.

When Mr. Flanders began missing more than hitting, almost falling down several times, he shoved the boy away and stomped toward the door. He turned around once to yell something more and point an angry finger at Zack, who lay weeping in the snow. The man slammed the door behind him. Momentarily it opened up again, and a teddy bear flew out at least twenty feet before burying its head in the snow.

Alex noticed his own pale face reflected in the glass. His mouth hung slightly open in astonishment. His legs were trembly.

The back door opened again, and the girl named Patience was shoved out as well, crying. The door slammed shut as if for the last time ever.

Alex retreated from the window to the landmarks of his room: the orange desk with its piles of papers and globe, the stereo system and all the CDs scattered around, the wild animal posters on the walls, his hockey equipment thrown in a jumble in the closet, the clothes hanging out of the dresser drawers, a teddy bear, brightly colored Lego pieces on the floor.

He went back to the window after a moment, thinking that the kids would be back inside. They weren't. They just sat out there and bawled.

He pulled on clean jeans and a shirt and padded out into the den in his bare feet.

"Dad," he said. His father looked up sleepily from the television.

After initially resisting interfering in other people's business, his father went to the Flanders' house to speak with the parents. When he returned, however, it was with Zack and Patience. He looked grim.

"They won't answer the door," he said to Alex's mother.

The kids stood wordlessly, soundlessly, in the foyer. The melting snow was making dark spots on the red carpet, but for once Alex's mother didn't seem to mind. She and his father argued in low voices just out of earshot—something about the police. Zack noticed Alex standing there in his bare feet, just staring at them. Neither of them knew what to say, so no one said anything.

Alex's mother returned.

"Well," she said kindly, "why don't we get you out of those wet clothes and into something warm?" She helped them take off their shoes.

"Do you guys want to sleep over here tonight and we can sort this out in the morning?" she asked kindly, as if they had shown up by invitation for a slumber party. Patience nodded shyly, and Zack shrugged his shoulders.

"Sure," he said. "Can I play the Nintendo?"

Alex's mother laid his sleeping bag out on the floor for Zack to sleep in, and dug out his father's old pajamas for Zack to wear. Patience would sleep on the cot in his parents' bedroom.

Alex sat on the edge of his bed and watched Zack change.

"They smell old," Zack said, sniffing the pajamas. "Like my gramma's."

He pulled off his shirt, and Alex saw he was branded with black-and-blue marks on his back and chest. Zack stopped and looked at Alex looking at him.

"Hey, thanks for being my friend," he said. He extended a hand, formally.

When have I been your friend? Alex wanted to say, but didn't. He wanted to laugh at the stupidity of it, but didn't. Couldn't, out of guilt, shame, and pity. So even though it made his heart sink, he took Zack's hand and shook it unenthusiastically. He thought about how he would have to walk the tightrope between his friends in the neighborhood and this stray boy to whom it was now impossible for him to be mean. Or even indifferent, maybe. None of the others would understand, even if he described what he had seen. He thought he could defend Zack to his friends and lose their respect, or not defend him and lose—he couldn't quite say what. He didn't think Zack's friendship was what he was worried about losing; it was something else, something he couldn't name but that he felt he would regret losing all the same. Something perhaps more valuable than the respect of his friends. Thinking about this problem made his stomach knot up.

The twinkly look in Zack's eyes seemed to say, Gotcha.

Years later there would be a blazing hot summer day by the lake. He and Zack would be fooling with the fishing tackle on the porch, cold drinks nearby sweating from the humidity.

Zack would look up all of a sudden and take in the scene before them. The children down in the water, pushing one another around in plastic inner tubes and making a lot of noise; their wives sitting on the end of the dock lazily swooshing their bare feet in the cool water, laughing now and then. The sun coming down on all of them. Three white pines by the shore, lofting magnificently toward the sky and rooted strongly, deep into the soil. The dog sleeping in the green shade.

"Who ever knew when we first met as kids that it would all come to this," Zack says in mild wonderment, and the memory of that Christmas vacation is awakened in Alex.

Mysterious, Alex thinks, that something as lowly as a moment's meager bit of pity would be the seed that grows into something you never expected at all when you planted it. Strange how our friendship, and all of us gathered here on this sunny day, could grow out of that cold winter, he thinks.

"Yeah," Alex says. "Who ever knew?"

Sign Language

The call came in the middle of the night during a strange dream Maggie was having about a blizzard of warm snow that covered and erased everything, making her the small center of a vast white ocean in which she struggled to keep from drowning. Great drifts moved past like herds of whales. Through the silence she heard the distant sound of a telephone ringing somewhere. Anxious to answer before the caller hung up, she pushed through the snow and cotton sheets to grab blindly for the phone on her nightstand. She slowly assembled the words of the calm woman on the other end: father, hospital, cardiac arrest.

"He asked that we call you," the woman said.

"Because he knew mom wouldn't have," Maggie said drowsily.

"What?"

"Nothing."

The nurse explained that although he was stable now, they would keep him overnight for observation and more tests.

But the next day, after a hard day of wait-ressing, Maggie called the hospital again and was told the doctors had scheduled her father for emergency heart bypass surgery the following morning. She called work to get the day off, and thought about leaving Aaron at a friend's, but then decided to bring him along.

They woke well before dawn. Aaron sat drowsing on the edge of the bed as she dressed him. She wanted to get an early start; it was a long drive to Saint Louis.

You look like you slept on your head, she told him, but his eyes were half-shut so he never even noticed. The car heater didn't work, and it was the middle of January, so she grabbed the comforter from her bed to cover them on the long drive. Aaron enter-tained himself by drawing abstract pictures in the window frost with the tip of a finger that he had poked through a hole in his mit-ten. He watched the passing scenery through the designs: scrubby trees and brush in frozen brown fields. Maggie passed the time worrying about her father—who had always blanched at the sight of her skinned knees and now was going to have his chest sawed open. She wished for a cigarette. She'd given them up when she got pregnant with Aaron, but the old urge always came back when she got stressed out.

At the hospital Maggie found her mother sitting on the edge of an emerald green high-backed armchair in the surgical waiting room, which was full of velvets and dark woods and artsy prints, as well as the requisite television with the sound turned down low and coffee table crowded with old copies of *People* and *Time* magazines. Her mother's anxious oval face was raised in rapt attention to a nurse who was offering reassurance in a creamy, patient voice. The tableau they presented was that of a medieval saint receiving a message from an angel of God.

Except her mother was no saint, and whatever she was being told apparently didn't satisfy her because she cut the nurse off abruptly.

"I know thousands of heart bypass operations are performed every year," she said, "but what I want to know are the odds. What are his chances?"

"That depends on the individual patient, Mrs. Mullins," the nurse replied. "Didn't Dr. Oui review the heart bypass procedure with you and your husband last night?"

Her mother snorted contemptuously, a habit left over from her school board days that Maggie found still made her cringe. "Yes, but I'd have to attend medical school to interpret his explanation. I know you medical people think it's best not to overwhelm us laymen with actual information, but I am a grown woman and I think I have a right to know what the odds are of my leaving this hospital a widow. The least you could do is tell me what the operation involves."

The nurse sat down on the edge of the chair opposite her mother and indicated where the doctors would saw open her husband's chest, how they would spread his ribs, deflate his lungs, hook him up to a special machine that would pump his blood, and then stop his heart.

"Stop the heart?" Her mother blanched and grabbed the nurse's arm.

"Only temporarily," the nurse said quickly. "They'll jump-start it again when they've fixed it. But they have to stop it while they're grafting the vein they'll take from his leg to the aorta—uh, that's like a big tube going out of the heart. There will be scars, of course, and he'll need a few months of rehabilitation after the surgery. Our nutritionist will review his dietary needs with you. We have a very high success rate for bypass surgery here, Mrs. Mullins. Besides, your husband seems to have a lot of fight in him."

The older woman let out a low moan and fell back into the chair. "James? James has about as much fight in him as a bug squashed on a windshield. He is going to die," she said melodramatically, "leaving me all alone in the world."

"You'll always have me," Maggie said brightly to announce her presence. "And Aaron." She tugged off his coat and took him by the hand.

"As I was saying, leaving me all alone," her mother repeated, not looking at Maggie at all. "Aside from my only grandchild, who I have not seen for three years and probably would not have seen ever again if it weren't for James."

Maggie sighed. "Here we go," she muttered under her breath.

"I did my best to raise a respectful child," her mother told the nurse. "I hope you never have the sort of children who back talk to their mother. It will break your heart. Mark my words."

Maggie learned from the nurse that her father had been in surgery for two hours, and that it was expected to take at least five hours. That left just three hours, but it may as well have been an eternity to Maggie— not only because her father's life hung in the balance but because she would have to spend it in the same room with her mother. The nurse indicated they had given her mother a tranquilizer to calm her down, which was a relief. But still . . . Maggie recalled the rare phone conversations they'd had in the seven years since she left home. These usually ended after less than five minutes when one or the other of them hung up in disgust. Her father, on the other hand, was as sweet as ever. He'd even come to Aaron's baptism alone, one of the few times he had defied her mother.

After the nurse left, Maggie seated herself on the couch and took out a tissue to wipe Aaron's runny nose. His big brown eyes were fixed on her mother, who was pretending to ignore them by burying her nose in an old issue of *People*. A woman on the television was expressing delight at the moisturizing qualities of a new dish soap.

Your grandmother, Maggie signed to him. He raised his eyebrows, interested. He walked over and tapped her on the knee. She lowered her magazine and gazed at him.

You're my grandmother, he said, smiling broadly. Then he climbed up into her lap, and she let him. She seemed astonished.

"What is he saying?"

"He's just introducing himself." Maggie smiled faintly; for once, her mother was left speechless.

She touched the boy's damp hair. "Hello, Aaron," she tried finally. "You're getting to be such a big boy. How old are you now?"

"He can't understand you."

"I thought all deaf children read lips," her mother said. "I saw a special on PBS about it."

"Eventually he'll learn, but it takes practice. The school he's going to believes in teaching American Sign Language before teaching how to read lips, to preserve deaf culture."

"Sounds like so much politically correct nonsense," her mother remarked. "I can't even speak to my own grandchild."

Maggie rolled her eyes. You were never very good at talking to me, either, she wanted to say; but instead she hunkered down on the floor in front of them and interpreted: *Show grandmother how old you are.*

He held up four fingers, then corrected himself and held up five. He made several small gestures toward her, raising his eyebrows expectantly.

"He wants to know how old you are," Maggie said.

Her mother laughed shortly: "Too old," she said, and then had an idea. She held up five fingers again and again, until she reached sixty-five. Aaron's eyes widened, and he exaggerated the sign for "old," extending it out away from him and letting his hand drop in exhaustion.

"Oooold," Maggie said, laughing. "He must have picked that up from one of his teachers at school."

"Teach me some words," her mother said. "Something simple that won't aggravate my arthritis. So I can talk with him."

Maggie paused, taken aback at the unexpected good mood, which she doubted would last very long. But she began with the manual alphabet anyway, and enlisted Aaron's help to show her mother the colors, the words for *bathroom, boy, girl, friend, beautiful, happy, eat, big,* and *understand,* among others. Aaron patted her on the hand excitedly and put his thumb on his chin, extending his index finger upward and then curling it down.

"That means 'who,'" Maggie said, smiling in anticipation of his little joke. He put his thumb on the tip of his nose and repeated the gesture.

"'Who knows?' Get it? It's like a pun. He's making the 'who' on his nose, so 'who knows.'"

Understanding slowly dawned on her mother's face, and she laughed and laughed. With Maggie's help she made the sign for "funny."

"I think he likes me," she said. "It's a shame you keep him from me."

Maggie's face darkened. "I do not keep him from you, Mother. You didn't want anything to do with him in the first place."

"I never said that!"

"No, your exact words were, 'It's a scandal on the family.'" Maggie put her arms around Aaron, who silently watched their faces. Sometimes she thought it was a blessing he was deaf.

"You're putting words in my mouth. Not that I approved of you running off with that boy and getting pregnant. You don't expect me to approve of that, do you? I told you that boy was no good. Did you listen? No," she said icily. She lowered her voice, conscious of the nurses they could hear chatting down the hall. "You never listened. Too busy thinking about yourself."

Maggie threw up both hands. "Stop! Just stop! Why do we have to get into this every time? That was seven years ago, Mom. Seven years! Most people would at least forget about it and find something positive to say after seven years, but here we are, still fighting like we were when I was sixteen."

"I'm not the one who brought it up," her mother said imperiously.

"You—" Maggie started, then threw up her hands again and stalked back to the couch. "Let's just not talk about it at all."

"Fine."

"Good."

Maggie picked up a magazine and flipped through celebrities' wedding pictures; they were all smiling. She would never escape her

mother's judgment, could never be good
enough in her mother's eyes. Besides,
Maggie was better at kicking herself for that
mistake named Michael than her mother ever
would be. The summer after graduation she
had been a counselor at a camp for kids with
disabilities; Michael had worked with the
deaf kids. His elegant communication with
them was nothing like the blunt barking of
the hearing world, and she was enchanted.
Ballet of the hands, he called it; so romantic.
Sometimes she wondered whether she had
confused falling in love with sign language
for falling in love with him, because it took
her two years to hear what he was actually
saying to her with those hands, two years of
waitressing while he attended Gallaudet
University, and then his sudden departure a
week after she told him she was pregnant
and keeping the baby: the slap-in-the-face
sign.

But the trouble with her mother preceded
all of that, and perhaps even led to it. Maybe
she wouldn't have left home if they hadn't
fought practically every weekend. Over parties. Boys. Clothes. Breakfast cereal. Anything at all. Maybe she wouldn't have gone
with Michael if her mother hadn't made her
stop seeing Brian the summer before, just
because she saw empty beer cans in the
back of his truck.

Maybe, maybe, maybe.

She closed her eyes and noticed she was bouncing her foot rapidly up and down—one of those habits that her mother had always nagged about. She would hear, "Don't be a nervous Nellie" for the rest of the days of her life. She forced it to stop.

She put down the magazine. Aaron had fallen asleep leaning against her mother, who was sleeping, too, head tilted back, mouth hanging open just a little. Her mother looked almost peaceful when she was asleep. Like one of those happy domestic moms in the dish soap commercials, except older. Her hair was grayer now, and her face looked as worn as the dried-out Play-Doh Aaron was always forgetting to put away.

Dear Lord, she said, *I'm so tired of always fighting with her.* She signed this, absently, a habit she had picked up from helping Aaron with his bedtime prayers every night. She often hoped that perhaps God's silences were just him signing back, although if he was, she had never seen it. *Why did you make Aaron deaf, when it's Mom and me who don't hear each other? We're deaf and we're mute, too. We have no peace except when there's silence between us. Would a little of the mud you used on that blind man's eyes work a miraculous cure on our ears, our tongues, our hearts?*

Nothing but questions. She had memorized a Scripture passage after learning that Aaron was as deaf as his father: "Who gives one man speech and makes another deaf and dumb? . . . Is it not I, the Lord? Go, then! It is I who will assist you in speaking and will teach you what you are to say."

Her mother suddenly started awake with a great yelp, knocking Aaron over and making Maggie jump upright in her chair. Her eyes were wide from some nightmare vision, and they scanned the room frantically, coming to rest on the clock.

"It's been six hours," she exclaimed, gripping the arms of the chair tightly and hyperventilating. "Something's wrong."

Maggie tried to be reassuring, although what she felt was annoyed. "They said it might take longer than five hours, Mom."

The old woman turned her head to stare at Maggie. She seemed to be seeing something else, remembering. "I had a dream," she said. "I had a dream that I was at home, asleep. That when I woke up James was there beside me. He always wakes up first, to make the coffee, except when he's sick. But he wasn't sick, he was cold, very cold. He wouldn't wake up. . . ." She began to cry. "I know something went wrong."

Maggie bit her lower lip and went over and took her mother's hand. "You've got yourself all worked up over nothing," she said. "Sshh, you'll get the nurses over here and they'll want to give you another tranquilizer."

Aaron sat on the floor, blinking the sleep from his eyes. Maggie handed her mother a Kleenex, not knowing what more to say. She had never seen her cry like this.

"I don't want to be alone," her mother said, sniffling.

"You're not going to be alone," Maggie said. "Let me go ask a nurse what's happening."

As it turned out, her father had been out of surgery for forty-five minutes and was already in the intensive care unit. Somehow they'd forgotten to tell Maggie or her mother. When Maggie told her mother the good news, she started crying all over again out of relief.

I'm hungry, Aaron said after they had sat there awhile waiting to be let in to see James.

His grandmother perked up, remembering the sign from her crash course earlier. "So am I," she said. "Wait . . . I always carry a snack with me, in case of emergency. Especially in the winter. You never know when you might get caught in a blizzard."

She rummaged around in the clutter of her large purse until she finally found a couple of battered-looking candy bars. She took one and broke it in three equal parts, carefully handing pieces to Maggie and Aaron.

"Take this and eat it," she said, making the sign for "eat" to Aaron. Just like a mother, Maggie thought; always ready to feed you.

It was snowing when they finally left the hospital, late that afternoon. The sun was shining just above the horizon, slanting through the flakes that floated down, filling the air with a lambent white glow.

"You two should have winter boots," her mother chided. "You'll catch a cold. You would never wear them as a girl, though, so I don't know why you would now."

Maggie checked her tongue against the words that rose in her throat. The snow was so beautiful, she thought. Manna from heaven must have looked like this, the frosty breath of angels dancing down to the earth.

"It's true," Maggie said. "Those blizzards come up out of nowhere. Floods, too, where we live down by the river. It's good to be prepared for acts of God like that."

"That's right," her mother responded, taking Aaron's hand, as the wind made glittering swirls all around them.

The Evolution of Dating

When you are six you are told by the second graders (who are authorities on the subject, being 15 percent older than you) that when you are on the swings and you fall into the same rhythm as the boy next to you (his toes and your toes touching lightly against the blue sky at the same time, like dancers), it means someday you'll be married.

And you believe it. During recess you find yourself on the swings, slyly trying to achieve the same rhythm as Adam Zinger, who is the cutest boy in the first grade. It doesn't matter to you that his last name is the same as a certain brand of cream-filled chocolate snack cake, which causes other kids to snicker during attendance. You are above things like that.

You would think that getting your swing lined up with his would be easy, but it turns out it's not. It's a complicated algebraic equation that you won't learn until physics class eleven years later, by which time you will have forgotten you ever had a use for it, even if you still play on swings. You move your legs faster, rushing at the ground, then curving back into the sky toward the top of the arc, where you balance weightlessly for the blink of an eye before falling back again. You steal sidelong glances at him, wondering if he no-tices what you are trying to do, wondering whether he is secretly conspiring to match his swing to yours. (Then you worry: What if he is, and you're slowing down just as he's trying to speed up, or vice versa?)

Curl your legs under yourself and tip your flying body so you can watch the grass race past. Hope that you will wind up next to him by chance. When you do, pretend not to notice. You fly like strong birds, like Canada geese headed south.

And then he leaps off the swing and goes screaming off toward a bunch of other boys who have found a kickball. Watch him go, his dirty shoelaces slapping at his tennis shoes. Keep swinging. Swing for the rest of recess if need be. Kick hard at the sky, as if you could crack its shell.

When recess is finally over, you feel sick from swinging too much and throw up in the hallway. As you lay on the cot in the nurse's office, it does not occur to you that this could be a metaphor for what it is like to be in love. You are only six, after all.

Pop quiz: Did God create a soul mate for you? Does love unfold as it does in storybooks? Or is true love merely a matter of chance? Why or why not? Ponder this often.

The first time a guy asks you out on a real date, you go to the zoo. This is how you are asked out: You are sitting at home innocently struggling with your math homework (story problems dealing with probability: "If the odds of your parents meeting and getting married were one in one hundred, and the odds of their parents meeting and marrying were also one in one hundred, what were the odds, before your grandparents met, of you eventually being born?") when your mother calls you to the phone.

"It's a boy," she says.

He says (in a nervously breezy way), "Hi, this is Anthony." You are thinking, "Who?" when he adds, "From school." Then you remember: Freckles, red hair, glasses, sort of quiet, plays hockey. Of course he asks you out. You hesitate. You don't know whether you actually want to go out with him—he's not the one you have a crush on—but then again, you don't *not* want to go out with him, so you say yes.

He seems surprised at this.

Your mother gives you a quarter and tells
you that if he tries anything inappropriate
(she offers a specific example: "french kiss-
ing"), you should give him the quarter and
tell him to call your father to ask if it's okay.
This, she says, will discourage him.

You roll your eyes and point out that you
are fourteen. You say: "We're going to the
zoo, Mom. The *zoo!*" She insists you take
the quarter anyway.

On the day of the date, a freak spring blizzard hits, so you are confined to the indoor
exhibits: the aquariums and the reptile
house, which smells like rotting leaves.

This would not be so bad, except that
Anthony tries very, very hard not to do or
say anything stupid. While he succeeds in
not appearing stupid to you, your conversation is about as exciting as the little signs
explaining the zoo exhibits: polite, to the
point, with short sentences, short para-
graphs, and lots of white space.

Long, quiet, uncomfortable white space.

At the gecko exhibit you watch two lizards
sitting perfectly still on a log, looking at each
other or looking at you and Anthony—it's
hard to tell, because they're so still they
could be fake. You notice Anthony's reflection in the glass, his eyes staring straight
ahead. Just like a gecko.

You wish you could grab him by the shoulders, look him in the eyes, and say: "I don't bite, okay? So relax! Have fun! *Loosen up!*" Somehow you instinctively know that this would backfire, so instead you talk about symbiosis in reptiles.

Be gentle. When you stand awkwardly in front of his house after it is over, say, "Well, there you be," and thank him for a nice time. When he is gone, wonder what your mother was worried about.

Your college roommate quotes from Rita Rudner's *Guy Guide:* "A good place to meet a man is at the Laundromat. These men usually have jobs and bathe." Vow not to resort to the Laundromat ever, even if it means never washing your clothes again.

In college you go to a lot of parties, where you meet a lot of guys. At one party, you escape the smoke and noise by climbing out onto the roof with a guy who plays the saxophone in a jazz band. He is two years older than you; he has this rich, low voice and an easy way of talking; his eyes are a dusky brown. As he sits with his back against the chimney, the profile of his face lit by the yellow halo of the streetlight, he tells funny stories about himself. He talks about wanting to change the world, but also about the importance of being realistic, which is why he believes in community activism. He says (looking up at you suddenly, as if he has only just realized this): "You know, you're just like this painting I saw the other day, this woman in a painting. Renoir, I think. If I could paint, I'd want to paint you. Maybe I'll learn, so I can." He smiles.

In a dim corner of your mind, a small thought counsels skepticism and caution. Your heart, however, has no doubt whatsoever that you are the first woman to move him to such poetry. Believe your heart. Allow it to track down the small thought of skepticism in your mind and kill it.

In the next few weeks, he teaches you to play pool and introduces you to his friends. He orders pizza to be sent to your room as a surprise while you're studying for finals, with poetry taped to the box cover. He serenades you by playing his saxophone under your window, music that sounds like a dark and mysterious river. No one in the building seems to mind that it's one in the morning.

Someday soon he will caress your cheek and say: "If you love me, then what's the problem?" or "But you're so beautiful. . . ."

This is how it will go:

You: "I don't think that's a good idea."

Him *(disguising his sarcasm as teasing):* "Loving me isn't a good idea?"

You: "Michael . . . I'm just not ready for this."

Him *(after a pause):* "I guess I thought you were mature enough."

(Long pause. Don't panic.)

(Don't cry.)

You *(softly):* "Do you really love me? Then don't ask me to do this. And don't be mad at me for saying no. Okay?"

(He will regard you seriously for a moment.)

Him: "Okay."

(Silence.)

Him: "Look, I should get going. It's late."

He will kiss you—on the cheek—and walk out. When he does, know in your gut that even if he calls you tomorrow, he has just left for good.

(Cry now.)

In the deepest recesses of your heart lies a truth your mind hasn't fully held yet, and this is it: What you really desire is a love that is deep and pure and full, a love far and beyond what any man can give you. You desire the love of

God, to fill you to overflowing and to make you strong and whole and full of happiness.

But the love of one guy who isn't a jerk would be all right, too, just about now.

Jockeys, race-car drivers, airplane pilots, slalom skiers, skydivers, tightrope walkers, and mountain climbers seek risk in order to know more fully that they are alive. This is why you keep dating.

Your best friend says: "What do you mean, 'Where are all the good guys?' Didn't you hear God stopped production on them in 1981?" Later she says: "I found a good guy once. He got accidentally run over by a truck, though."

Three short-lived relationships and two blind dates later, you contradict your best friend by meeting a nice guy through work. He holds doors for you. Napoleon, your cat, takes a liking to him immediately. He brings you flowers on your first date. He smiles often and lies about your cooking. Your parents are impressed by him, especially your dad, who spends an hour talking with him about golf, the stock market, and quack grass.

The love you share with him is the easily domesticated kind, and it becomes as comfortable as a faithful old dog, happy to see you every time you come home. You share the vocabulary of two people who take their eventual marriage for granted: You talk of interest rates on thirty-year mortgages, you debate the best way to raise children, and when you decide to get a new car, he comes shopping with you.

All of which leaves you full of simple bliss when you are twenty-three. When you are twenty-four, however, you notice a subtle shift in your attitude toward him, marked by small tremors deep below the surface of your relationship. You notice that you laugh at jokes he only smiles at, that in fact he seems to wince when you laugh so loudly in public places that people turn to look. And you, for your part, find yourself zoning out when he gets all enthusiastic explaining the stock market and real estate; you only half listen, thinking about something entirely different—whether his small (but surprisingly annoying) habit of drumming his fingers over and over when he gets anxious is a trait your children might inherit, for instance.

These are little things, but as they are multiplied several times over, they point to something larger: a hidden fault line between you, where he moves one way and you move another. You sense a danger lurking there. Your subconscious warns that as the two of you move closer, the small tremors could become larger. You feel anxious and harassed, like an animal before an earthquake.

On your twenty-fifth birthday, he throws you a surprise party. You are surprised, but not as much as when you open a small white box wrapped in a red ribbon to find his present to you is an engagement ring. Suddenly he's kneeling in front of you, his innocent face turned up toward yours, vulnerable to your thirty guests. What will you say? People are smiling rapturously; eyes are misting up. So lie. Say yes, and explain later.

What will you tell him? Well, who knows? You'll wing it, trying to point out how these small personality differences seem to indicate larger ones, scarier ones. He won't understand, of course, your clumsy explanations of relationship seismology.

You will spend months trying to explain how the emotional topography of your relationship has changed since its beginning. He will feel scorned, and hurt, and will be bitter. Accept this. He will be angry and accusing, then weepy and pleading. Resist this. (Remember the divorces of your friends' parents.) Your ability to cause him as much pain as if you'd taken a knife to him will make you dizzy and awed, and the empty space he leaves, ironically, will make you cry. How do you know you've done the right thing? Imagine yourself walking down the aisle to marry him. If it gives you a sick feeling of impending doom, you've done the right thing.

Your mother says: "Think of this as a learning experience. Think of this as an opportunity for personal growth. Think of this time of independence as a place to develop your own sense of identity and self-worth."

Promise her you will.

Practice for the single life. This is what you learn: You can paint your own portrait, not as well as Renoir, but probably better than Michael ever could. Running a marathon is not as hard as you thought. When going to a restaurant alone, it helps to bring a book to read while waiting for your food to come. You can call your best friend in the middle of the night, and she won't hang up on you. Your closest male friend can say, "Statistically speaking, women over age thirty have a greater chance of getting killed in a car accident than getting married," and you can say in return, "So, what's your point?" and mean it.

On a Tuesday in May, you put a dollar's worth of quarters in the machine at the Laundromat (yes, it has come to this—deep down, you knew it would, didn't you?) and press the start button, but nothing happens. So you go over to the attendant (a sweaty woman who smells like soap and watches television behind the counter), who explains that they raised the rates to a dollar and a quarter last week, but haven't gotten around to changing the signs on the machines. You want to ask her what you're supposed to do, since you just poured liquid detergent all over your clothes, and you can't just leave them there to go home for another quarter. But her gaze has already drifted back to the television, so instead you return to the machine, ticked off. You find it running in the wash cycle.

"I had some extra change, so . . ." He looks a little embarrassed—*sheepish*, you think—but at first glance he doesn't appear to be a serial murderer, so you smile. "I hope you don't mind," he says.

Tell him you don't mind. Offer to let him use your detergent so he doesn't have to buy his own. Laugh self-consciously and make jokes about being in a laundry detergent commercial.

"The whites are so, so—white!" he says in mock amazement, raising his eyebrows as he holds up a T-shirt.

Later, hope that by chance he's walking home in your general direction. Be nonchalant when it turns out he is. When you part ways, tell him to watch out for trucks.

Wash your clothes about three times more than normal over the next couple of weeks. Don't mention him when your roommate asks about your new obsession with clean clothes. Tell her you're so amazed by the new and improved Tide that you need to wash your clothes again and again. Ignore her when she stares at you for giggling at this.

Walking home from the laundry one warm June night, the two of you take the long way past the elementary school. You set down your laundry baskets and drift over to the playground. You have been talking about everything—the difficulty of finding decent-paying jobs with a liberal arts degree, being afraid of your parents dying someday, how weird your cat is, music. (The *Guy Guide* says that men who listen to classical music tend not to spit.)

Try not to think about the fact that the things you say now could change the rest of your life. Don't wonder if he's the one; maybe he is, maybe he isn't. Hold your breath instead.

You find yourselves on the swings. Although both of you swing in tandem, your toes pointing at the stars at the same time, you do not remember that this is supposed to foretell marriage—it has been a long time since first grade. You do not think about the future because you are holding fast to this moment, even as your swings imitate clock pendulums measuring each moment's passing.

You don't keep swinging until you throw up. Instead, you gradually float back down to earth, and he starts pushing his swing toward yours, and you push yours away and around his. You circle each other teasingly, the chains making peculiar metallic noises as they wrap together above you. They draw you close even as they strain to untwist and send you spinning away.

Push your legs against the ground to hold you in place, and kiss.

Your clean laundry is blowing away in the breeze. Ignore it.

The Proposal

"Marry me," Scott said, and Emily at first thought he was teasing, so she just smiled at him and said, "All right. When?"

They were sitting on a bough of the plum tree in the backyard, spying on everything that was going on below. No one could see them up there, because they were hidden like birds in the leaves. But they could look down on all the people just fine, like angels maybe do from clouds. Emily's family, the Wilders, were having the reunion they pulled together whenever one of them got brave enough to take on the job of organizing it, and about 146 of them were there, with three babies on the way. The young kids were playing tag around a huge cottonwood tree, whose boughs shaded the picnic tables that had been drawn up underneath it, out of the sun. Men with potbellies sat around sipping light beer and arguing about football, while the boys home from college and some of the younger fathers actually played it in the pasture. The women talked in their own groups, or wiped the faces of protesting children.

Grandpa Wilder was telling jokes to Emily's cousins—Becky and Julie and Cassandra, the ones who were constantly talking about weddings (or so it seemed to Emily), even though they weren't even dating.

Emily took special note of her mother, snapping the lid on a Tupperware bowl full of pink fluff to keep the flies off, and her father, sitting off by himself in a lawn chair reading the paper. She marveled at the way they didn't even have to pretend to be getting along. Emily figured no one had noticed their indifference toward each other because everyone was used to them acting like that as a couple. And she had been worried that there would be a scene! She realized that if anyone did find out what was going on, they wouldn't be surprised—not like she was. The realization made her wonder why she'd been surprised at all. They lived under her nose for more than twenty years; shouldn't she have seen this coming?

"Em," Scott was saying, gently touching her face with his index finger to turn her attention back to him. "You've been so day-dreamy today. Your head's in the clouds."

"I'm sorry," she said. "There's been so much going on."

He looked down past his dangling feet at the ground. "Maybe this wasn't the best time to do this."

"Do what?"

"To propose to you," he said. "I just asked you to marry me. I thought this would be a nice place to pop the question, where we kissed first . . . I was going to wait until tonight, but it slipped out early. I couldn't help it. It must be the heat, or something in the punch." He shrugged and gave her the boyish smile that sometimes made her heart flip-flop.

Emily's mouth opened once, then shut again. She was speechless.

"You're serious!" she said finally.

"Yes, ma'am," he said, then reached into his pocket and pulled out a small box covered in emerald green velvet. "I even brought this to prove it."

She opened it and there was the fabled ring, the real article—not the fake plastic rings she and her next-door neighbor used to play wedding when they were kids. She took it out and put it on her finger.

Scott was grinning. He knew what her answer would be; they'd been talking about getting married for at least two years now. She'd expected him to propose formally in the fall, though, after he was out of college for good.

"Well say something! The suspense is killing me!" Scott said.

Emily looked up from the ring, and tears were running down her face. "Yes, yes—yes,

I will marry you," she said, and she started crying outright. Then she leaned over to embrace him and fell out of the tree.

Grandpa Wilder, who always boasted that he had eyes like a hawk, shouted something and came running over, which attracted the attention of everyone else.

"I'm fine," Emily kept saying, first to Scott and then to Grandpa Wilder. Fortunately the grass under the tree hadn't been mowed, so her landing was softer than it might have been. But when she tried to stand up, pain shot up her leg and made her wince, and she sat right down again. Her face hurt where a branch had raked across it. She still clutched the ring box, though.

"What happened? What were you doing up there?" Grandpa Wilder asked all at once, kneeling in the grass in his good pants to feel her ankle.

"K-I-S-S-I-N-G," one of the eight-year-olds said delightedly. Quite a little crowd had gathered, Emily saw, including her mother.

"Scott proposed to me," she said.

"He did!" her grandpa exclaimed. He glanced up from her ankle, his concerned face suddenly beaming.

"And did you say yes?" her mother asked.

Just then her grandpa moved her foot the wrong way, and Emily yelped.

"Yes she did," Scott put in, squeezing her hand. "I didn't think she would fall out of the tree, though, or I would have proposed the old-fashioned way, on the ground. Sorry, Em."

"Don't be sorry," she said. She wiped a little trickle of blood from her face. "It was more romantic in the tree."

"Well, at least you'll have a story you can entertain people with for the rest of your life," Grandpa Wilder said. "But for now we better have that ankle looked at."

"This is so exciting," her mother said, and Emily could see that she was already scheming about the wedding.

At the clinic the doctor, the nurse, and the X-ray technician, upon hearing her story, all made the same joke: "You really fell for him, didn't you?" Emily realized she would probably be hearing that joke for the rest of her life.

Fortunately the ankle was sprained, not broken; she got a pair of crutches and orders to stay off her foot and out of trees. When she returned, with Grandpa Wilder and Scott walking on either side of her to make sure she didn't fall, people stood up and clapped like they do when an injured player gets up and walks off the field. They set her up on a lawn recliner and brought lemonade to her and generally treated her like royalty.

"So, congratulations, Champ," her father said, tapping her shoulder with his folded-up newspaper. He usually had a weathered, impassive face like a sea captain on the bridge of his ship, but now he was smiling slightly as he pulled up a lawn chair. Her mother was already sitting on the other side of her, and Scott was there, too, massaging her bare feet.

"Thanks," she said, smiling. She felt a little squirmy because her parents had been extra snippety with each other in the last few days, and her internal radar was warning her that any truce brought about by news of the en-gagement might not last long.

"When's the big day?" her mother asked.

"We haven't talked about that yet," Emily said.

"We didn't get much of a chance," Scott laughed, glancing at Emily accusingly.

"You've got to reserve the church and the reception hall fast," her mother was saying. "Minnie Jo was telling me that her daughter waited until four months before the wedding to rent a hall, and they couldn't find a single place in town. They had the wedding in Miesville, and the reception all the way over in Grange."

Her father scowled slightly. "There's plenty of time to worry about that. But what you should get going on is marriage preparation. You talk to Father Bill yet?"

"No," Scott said.

"Do that right away. I'd talk to him first thing Monday morning."

"There's no rush," her mother said.

"What do you mean?" her father asked. "Just a second ago you were talking about how important it is to reserve the church. I think marriage preparation is more important than reserving the church."

"Without a church, there won't be a wedding," her mother countered.

"If they're late reserving the church, they might not get married as soon as they want to. Without marriage preparation, their marriage might not last as long as they want it to."

It was unbelievable, Emily thought, that they were actually fighting over her engagement. They were ruining everything.

"All I'm saying," Emily's mother said, lowering her voice and glaring out of her pointed face, "is if there's enough time to reserve the church, there's enough time for marriage preparation."

Emily put her hands up to her head. She felt like the borderland between two warring countries. "This sets a new record, guys. Less than a minute of conversation before an argument. Oh, wait—we never really had a conversation, did we? Well, nice try anyway."

Her parents blinked at her in surprise, and there was an awkward moment of silence in which everyone's embarrassment was obvious. Scott was staring at Emily's ankles, and Emily's face got pink, because she'd never spoken back to her parents so brazenly before. When Emily was growing up, her parents didn't allow that kind of talk from her or her sisters. Emily thought: Here is something else that's going to change about our family.

"Well, I'm sorry," her father said. "I guess it just goes to prove my point about marriage preparation. Better that than marriage counseling." He stood up and walked away, leaving Emily and Scott with her mother, who looked like she was bravely trying not to cry.

"I'm sorry, too," her mother said, rubbing her hand against Emily's forehead like she used to do when Emily was sick. "I promise we'll try hard not to ruin your wedding. We'll be good."

Emily bit her lower lip. After a moment her mother stood up and excused herself. When she had left, Scott and Emily sat quietly. Scott resumed massaging her bare feet.

"This isn't turning out to be the happiest day of your life, is it?" he asked.

"Oh yes it is," Emily said. She said it so quickly and fiercely that, after a pause, they both burst out laughing a little.

"They're getting a divorce," she said, without thinking about it. There. She suddenly felt easier, now that he knew.

Scott's eyebrows shot up, and he gazed at her, thoughtful. "I didn't know that."

"I didn't either, until about five days ago. They're trying to keep it secret until after the reunion."

He leaned back on his elbows. "That bites. Em, I'm really sorry for you."

"Don't be sorry. If they want to get divorced, that's their business. I'm not going to let it ruin my life."

"Is that why you've been so distracted lately? Why didn't you tell me sooner? Because I wouldn't have proposed if I knew you were going through this."

Emily frowned. "That's why I didn't say anything. I was afraid . . . you know, that it would affect us."

"It doesn't change how I feel about you," Scott said. "I love you just as much, whether your parents are divorced or not."

"No, that's not what I mean," Emily said. She hesitated. "I guess I was afraid to bring it up because it does affect us. It changes things."

"How?"

"It makes me wonder whether the same thing could happen to you and me."

"No," Scott said, looking hard into her eyes. "No, it won't. We love each other."

Emily shook her head and leaned forward, intense. This was important; she'd been thinking about it in the doctor's clinic and on the ride home. "So did they. At least I hope they did, when they got married. You know what my mom told me the other day, when they told me about the divorce? She said sometimes love doesn't last. That people change, and they leave the love behind with who they used to be."

"You don't believe that, do you?"

"There's got to be some explanation for why so many people get divorced. Think of how many kids we know whose parents got divorced, or who never had two parents."

"A lot."

"That's what makes me wonder whether the same thing could happen to you and me. I don't think it will, but if people thought they would end up divorced, they wouldn't get married in the first place, right?"

"I don't know," Scott said, frowning. "Now you're making me worried."

"Don't be worried."

"First you say how do we know we won't get divorced, then you say don't worry about it. You're being confusing."

"Sorry."

"It's okay. Life gets more confusing all the time. But what are you really saying—that we shouldn't get married?"

Emily rubbed her eyes. "No, no," she said—"that's not what I'm saying at all." She was getting a headache from being in the sun, or from her parents, but she didn't want Scott to know that.

She had an idea.

"Help me up," she said. "I want to show you something."

They went inside the big old farmhouse and up the narrow staircase to Emily's grand-parents' bedroom. She pushed open the door and found her grandma lying on the bed.

"Oops," Emily said, but it was too late. Her grandma woke with a start. "I didn't mean to wake you up, Grandma. I just wanted to show Scott your pictures."

Her grandma stretched and yawned. "That's all right," she said, still lying on the bed. "I was just taking a little nap. All that cooking wore me out! But you can look at the pictures."

The walls were covered with pictures of the family from over the years. Most of them were black and white. There were pictures of birthday parties and weddings, and color pictures of small children—grandchildren and nieces and nephews, including a picture of Emily with short hair and a cherubic smile. One showed some of the men and boys smiling around a dead deer. In another, the kids picked through the wreckage of the barn that got destroyed by a tornado in '63; the farmhouse stood intact in the background. There was a picture of Emily's Uncle Josie at age ten, too, the last picture of him before he was killed in a threshing machine. The whole wall was a montage of moments from the life of the family, and a testament to how it had grown and flourished.

"Here's my grandparents' wedding picture, from 1942, right before Grandpa went off to the war," Emily said. The happy couple in the picture looked no older than Emily and Scott. "They took this right down in the living room. They only took one picture, because they were too poor to afford any more. My grandpa was about to leave for overseas, and they didn't know if they would see each other again, so they got married pretty quick."

"That's right," Emily's grandma said from the bed. "Doesn't Grandpa look handsome?"

"Yes he does," Emily said, moving to another picture—this one of a woman holding a child by a bright window. "Here is a picture of my grandma holding my mom. She got pregnant right before Grandpa left for the war, and she had to raise my mom all by herself until he came back in 1945."

"This is interesting," Scott said. "But what does this have to do with what we were talking about before?"

"When I think of the way I want my marriage to be, I think of my grandparents," Emily said. "They're proof that it's not impossible."

"What?" Emily's grandma asked.

"Having a happy marriage."

"Oh," her grandma said.

"Scott proposed to me today."

"Oh!" Her grandma's mouth held the O shape for a second. "Congratulations. It's about time."

"Grandma, you went through lots of hard times," Emily said. "How did you manage to get through them all and stay married?"

Her grandma blinked her large eyes once or twice and scratched her head.

"Now that you mention it, I don't know how we got through all those hard times!" she exclaimed, laughing her funny laugh that always made Emily laugh, too. "That's something else, isn't it?"

"Grandma!" Emily said. "You're old! You're supposed to be wise! You're supposed to know the answers to questions like these!"

"That's a myth put out by the AARP," her grandma said with a mischievous smile.

"What's the AARP?" Scott asked.

"The American Association of Retired People," her grandma said. "They have a nice magazine."

"No, I'm serious," Emily said, reaching up to take her parents' wedding picture off the wall. "Look at how happy they are. Just like Scott and me. And now they're getting a divorce. And I don't even know why."

"It makes you mad, doesn't it?" her grandma asked.

"Yes it does. It makes me mad because they didn't try hard enough. It makes me mad because they've made me scared about getting married. I don't mean I'm scared of you, Scott. See? Now I'm insulting my fiancé."

Scott smiled. "I know what you mean."

"Well, if it makes you think about why you're getting married, maybe that isn't a bad thing," her grandma said. "Do you love each other?"

"Yes," Scott said, and Emily nodded.

Her grandma regarded them carefully, perhaps inspecting them to determine whether they were qualified to be married. The lines of her face seemed sympathetic, anyway.

"Emily, will you love Scott even when he gets fat, or if you find out he's lazy—now, don't take this personally, Scott, it's just an example—or if he gets in a bad car accident and you have to take care of him for the rest of his life?" she asked, and Emily seemed shocked at the thought.

"And Scott," her grandma continued, as if she were conducting a mock wedding with very strange vows right then and there, "will you love Emily even if she gets whiny and cranky in middle age, or if she loses her breasts to cancer like her Aunt Jan?"

They smiled nervously, not having thought of these possibilities before, but they glanced at each other conspiratorially and nodded anyway.

"Well, you think about it before you tie the knot," Emily's grandma said. "You really want to know how I think your grandpa and I got through all those hard times? When we got married, we decided that we would give our whole selves to each other the same way Jesus gave his whole life to us—even though we don't deserve it. See, if we'd decided to split the burdens fifty-fifty in our marriage, we would never have made it. I can tell you, I came close to leaving your grandpa after your Uncle Josie died."

"No way!" Emily said. "You did?"

"Yes," her grandma said. She paused a second. "Because for a long time, it was like living with a dead man. He blamed himself for Josie dying, so much that he almost forgot the rest of his family was still alive and needed him. It was hard. That's why I say I don't know how we got through some of those hard times. But I know that if God hadn't been part of our marriage, and if I hadn't been so stubborn about not giving up, we wouldn't have made it."

Later that evening Scott and Emily helped
her grandparents wash huge stacks of dirty
dishes in the steamy kitchen. Most of the relatives had gone home, including her parents.
When they were finished, and Emily had
kissed her grandparents good night, she and
Scott went outside into the cooling evening
air.

There were whole fields of stars set
against the black sky, so many more than
you could see in town. The stars out here
always gave Emily a powerful sense of the
whole world being held carefully in a soft
nest of light, like a fragile little egg.

"You looked so pretty, washing dishes,"
Scott said as he held her.

"I hope you don't have the idea that you're
going to have many chances to watch me
washing dishes."

"No, I always said I would help."

"I mean I think we should invest in a
dishwasher."

"That's got my vote."

They kissed for a little while.

"So," Scott said at last, as she traced the
curve of his neck with her fingers. "Is this
still the best day of your life?"

"Yes," Emily said.

"Because after we talked this afternoon, I
wasn't sure your 'yes' was still a 'yes.'"

"It is!" Emily said.

They listened to crickets and watched for meteors to make little exclamation points in the sky.

"What if I had said no?" Emily asked after a while.

Scott cleared his throat. He looked real serious. "I can't imagine that. I think it would be the most painful thing in my life. But I love you, so I would have to let you go, if that's what you really wanted."

Emily stared at him, amazed because what she was saw there in his face was true love, and she'd never comprehended its shape and form before. She imagined what he would look like in fifty years, and decided he would probably turn out to be one of those funny-looking old men with big ears and a big nose and a wide, toothy smile.

And she imagined a blank wall in their bedroom, slowly filling up with pictures from their life together, the good times and the bad. She saw it filling up and overflowing, until someday there would be no room left anywhere in their house to display the abundance of their love.

Sister Zoe, Meet the Gardener

A spirit from on high is poured out on us,
   and the wilderness becomes a fruitful field,
   and the fruitful field is deemed a forest.
Then justice will dwell in the wilderness,
   and righteousness abide in the fruitful field.
                                    (Isaiah 32:15—16)

Sister Zoe longed for the taste of food over the tongue—the tang of garlic and salt and tomato on a pizza, the mild creaminess of milk, the messy sweetness of an orange torn open with the teeth. Instead, the doctors nourished her evaporating body with clear liquids that dripped through tubes into her veins. They wouldn't let her near food, for fear she would choke. Nonetheless, she missed the soul of food, the taste of something other than her own dry mouth.

Her journey to death was becoming a long, solitary march through the desert. She waited for visions to come to her: long-dead relatives, angels, maybe Jesus or Mary. She knew such things were not uncommon as souls passed over into the new country, for many of the dying had reported the lay of the land to her as she kept vigil by their beds. A part of her hoped she, too, would experience an intrusion of the divine.

She had no heavenly visions. But as wakefulness came and went like a gentle, wandering wind, she did have dreams. For instance, she dreamt about the mischievous girl named Sulee, one of the many children she had taught during her missionary years in Africa. In this dream, the girl was lying in a pool of her own blood, stabbed through the gut with a machete. Sulee was not the first, and certainly not the last, to die in the ethnic violence that erupted all around Matate village, but she was the one Sister Zoe remembered long after her community had ordered her back to Iowa for her own safety. Perhaps it was the girl's bright yellow head scarf, or the gentle way she had with her younger siblings, so motherly for a nine-year-old.

She told Father Manion about the dream when he came to hold his own vigil at her bedside. He had been her student once, in the years before her retirement when she had taught high school algebra. His round, brown face still seemed young to her.

"Why do you think you're dreaming about Sulee now, twenty years later?" he asked.

"I've always felt guilty that we never buried her body," Sister Zoe said, coughing deeply—her lungs kept filling with fluid despite all medical efforts to keep the flood-waters at bay. "We left in such a hurry."

The priest raised his eyebrows and tilted his head to one side. "You feel guilty about abandoning her, you mean. Or for not preventing her death."

"Yes," Sister Zoe said. She folded her bony hands together over the white sheet.

"There is no reason for you to feel that way," he said. He spoke carefully, as if he were tasting each word. "It's not your fault she died."

"My head knows that, but not my heart," she said. "We were supposed to be the hands and feet of Jesus to those people, and we ran away when they needed us the most, in their suffering. We left so we'd be safe. But what for? Most of the women who were with me are just as dead now as they would have been then. I am dying now, too. We should have stayed. I should have at least buried the girl."

Her eyes had gone all teary. Father Manion reached across the bed and squeezed her hand but said nothing for a while.

"I'm sorry," she said.

"Don't be sorry."

"It's this place—it's got me down."

The priest nodded, handing her a tissue. "So. Have you had any good dreams?"

She thought about it. "Yes, I did. I dreamt about driving across the country to see the ocean when I was in college, with some friends. We slept on the beach in March, in our winter coats." Her eyes got dreamy. "I had cancer—it was usually fatal in those days—and I went with my friends to see the ocean, and to say good-bye to them. But I didn't want to die, so I prayed hard for a miracle. I promised God I would give my life to him if I survived."

"Obviously you did survive," Father Manion said. "A miracle?"

"I think so," Sister Zoe said. "The tumor disappeared."

"And that's when you chose the religious life?"

Sister Zoe laughed, which made her cough raspily. She nodded as she caught her breath. "I thought that the only way you could give your life to God was by becoming a nun, which caused problems years later when I realized the truth. But I worked through those, and stayed."

"And are you glad you did?"

"Yes," she said, the word sharp on her tongue, and the look in her eyes suddenly strong. "Yes. When I think of what an abundant life it's been, it takes my breath away. It has opened my eyes to a million miracles."

Later in the day, her community and her other friends gathered around her bed, a hot beam of afternoon sun slanting through the window at them. When Father Manion began the anointing, they each placed a hand on her body in blessing. It was the most pleasant sensation, her body covered with warm hands all over. Sister Maribeth stroked her hair gently as Father Manion pressed oil to her forehead, then her hands, then her feet.

"May the God of all consolation bless you in every way and grant you hope all the days of your life. Amen.

"May God restore you to health and grant you salvation. Amen.

"May God fill your heart with peace and lead you to eternal life. Amen."

When it was over, she opened her eyes to all their faces. "Thank you," she said.

"Is there anything else we can do for you?" Sister Maribeth asked.

She was so tired; sleep was closing in on her like dusk. "Some spumoni ice cream would be heavenly."

Father Manion smiled. "We'll see what we can do."

During the night, she slept long and deep, and had powerful dreams. She swam up to awareness only as someone's hand rocked her dream-boat, pushing insistently at her shoulder.

"Wake up, wake up, wake up."

Zoe's eyes snapped open. It was a girl in a white nightgown with yellow butterflies print- ed all over it. She had large brown eyes. The girl turned her face sideways to see Zoe better.

"Hello," the girl said.

"Hello," Zoe said, blinking several times. The clock on the wall said it was five in the morning. "What room did you escape from?"

The girl leaned forward, until her beautiful brown face was inches from Zoe's. "I'm hun- gry," she whispered conspiratorially, her eyes widening. "Let's go find something good to eat."

Zoe laughed. Didn't they feed anyone around here? "I can't get you anything to eat. See, I'm stuck in bed. Go out in the hall and ask one of the nurses for a snack."

The girl shook her head solemnly and began removing Zoe's covers. "They don't have the good stuff. We want real food, right?" The girl took Zoe's arm and peeled away the tape holding the IV line in place.

"Hey, don't do that!" Zoe said.

The girl smiled brightly at her as she removed the needle and coiled up the line. "Why not? If you eat real food, you won't need it."

Zoe regarded the girl curiously for a moment. "It's not my job to feed you, you know."

The girl gave her a "get serious" look.

"Well," Zoe sighed. "Maybe I can get something to eat myself while I'm at it." She was suddenly hungry for strawberries in creamy yogurt.

She swung her feet over the edge of the bed and was surprised at how well she felt. She breathed in deeply; no coughing. The girl took her by the hand and led her to the door.

The hallway was full of people—patients mostly, in bathrobes and flimsy blue hospital gowns. Nurses guided the people along with words of encouragement and direction: "No, ma'am, you don't need discharge papers." "Yes, Mr. Priske, go down the hall and to your left. Just follow everyone else."

Zoe looked around in wonderment. "What's going on?" she asked. "Is there a fire or something?"

"No, there's no fire!" the girl laughed. She tugged Zoe into the hallway eagerly. "Everyone's hungry, that's all."

They followed the general flow of the crowd toward the elevators. At the nursing station, the nurses were shutting down computers and abandoning their posts. The vending machines they passed were empty;

candy bar wrappers were littered every-where, trampled underfoot like autumn leaves.

Zoe and the girl squeezed into the eleva-tor with some other patients. "Am I the only one around here who wants to know why we're evacuating a perfectly good hospital in the middle of the night?" Zoe asked them.

"Food," said a large, balding man wearing a red velvet robe and cow slippers. "I tell you, I own fourteen Shoney's family restau-rants in five states, so I know food, and this hospital food is the worst. They've had me on this no-fat, no-salt, no-nothing diet ever since my triple bypass heart surgery, and I mean, what's the point? Why bother?" He shook his head as the elevator doors opened on the lobby, and they joined everyone else heading outside. "I'm starving, and so is everyone else in this place. I feel like I haven't eaten in . . . in forty days, practi-cally. Even the nurses are sick of the food!"

"Amen to that," a passing nurse put in.

"So when we heard about how everyone's invited to this big party out in the country, we figured, why not? Sounds like the guy hosting this thing puts on quite a spread."

They passed through the sliding glass doors at the hospital entrance and found themselves on the street, which was lit by the pink and gold Easter colors of dawn.

"Looks like everyone had the same idea," Zoe said in amazement.

The street was filled with more people than Zoe had ever seen in downtown Des Moines. It was like a stage onto which the entire cast of some bizarre play had come out for the final curtain call. There were businesspeople in suits, Laotian dancers, kindergartners holding hands in a line, inner-city kids passing a basketball around, veiled Iranian women, several hundred South African soldiers, lots of shoppers with empty shopping bags—even the governor of Iowa, who waved and shook hands with passersby as if she were working a parade the day before elections.

The restaurateur folded his arms across his wide chest. "This is just great. I hope all the good stuff isn't gone by the time we get there."

"Oh, don't worry," the girl piped up. "He's rich enough to feed everyone, with leftovers to spare."

"Well, let's get going," the restaurant guy said, grunting and ambling into the crowd.

The girl tugged at her hand, but Zoe didn't follow. "Wait; just wait," she said. She was staring intently at the passing crowd. This mystery seemed familiar somehow, as if she should know what it was all about—but she didn't, and that bothered her. She directed her gaze to the strange young girl. "What's going on?"

"Come and see," the girl replied with a smile. "You're not afraid, are you?"

"No," Zoe said, a little taken aback. She'd been afraid before in life, but she had never given in to fear—except for perhaps when she left Matate village. "No," she said again, "but I don't even know where this thing is, or how to get there."

"Yes you do," the girl said.

A man with a crooked nose and sad, baggy eyes approached them. "Excuse me," he said, waving his hand at Zoe. "Can you help me find the way to this party?" He was awkwardly carrying shopping bags from various department stores, all of them stuffed full of boxes. He shifted his load and added, "All this shopping made me pretty ravenous."

"She knows the way," the girl said, looking up at Zoe expectantly. "Don't you?"

Zoe silently looked down at the girl for a moment. She looked back at the man and saw the hunger in his face. Something like understanding was dawning on her now, as she recognized the man's hunger, and the girl's simple joyfulness.

"Yes," she finally told him, slowly. Yes, she thought, she knew all about bravely entering mystery. "I think I do. You can walk with us."

"Oh—thanks!" the man said, readjusting his bags. "But—these boxes—uh, could you help carry some?"

"What's in them?" Zoe asked.

"Uh, clothes, mostly. Nothing that I can eat, which is what I really need."

"Well, I think I can help you out," Zoe said, noticing some of the underclad patients from the hospital. She winked at the girl, who covered her mouth and giggled.

They entered the motley parade behind a high school marching band. Zoe went through the man's new clothes as they walked along, and gave them all away to anyone who needed them. With his load lightened, the man traveled much more easily. He seemed pleasantly surprised that he didn't miss his baggage at all.

They walked east for a very long time, all the way out of the city. The girl skipped along, or chatted with different people. For a while the inmates of a maximum-security prison, still wearing their gray uniforms, took turns giving her rides on their shoulders so she could see above the crowd. Later, she and Zoe danced to the music of a passing mariachi band.

Zoe took in the faces of the people around her. She knew these people, and knew their hungers, from all those years of working in parishes and schools and in Africa. She was happy to be traveling again, and happier still to be traveling with them. She was at home here on the road with friends.

Soon they were well into the countryside, where fields rolled out all around them, black and ready for planting. People began leaving the procession and making their way across the fields toward a distant stream.

"Come on!" the girl said excitedly, jumping all around Zoe. "Let's run!"

Zoe laughed at the suggestion, because running for fun was a child's pastime, and she was no child—and she had on only hospital slippers, besides. But it had been a weird enough morning so far; who was to say she couldn't run?

So she did; haltingly at first, and then with confidence, exhilarated at the sensation of a wind of her own making on her face. She chased the girl, weaving around people who cheered them on, until they came to the edge of the stream. There, she caught the squealing girl and scooped her up. She spun around and thought of dunking her in the water—but then she saw a man watching them, and she stopped abruptly and stared, breathing hard from running; she thought she knew him.

He looked like the gardener of this place, a common farmer, because he wore faded, dirty overalls and a floppy wide-brimmed hat, and he was unshaven. And yet he did not look common at all. His bearing was such that she thought he might be the owner of the place, the host of the party. He was looking at her with an amused but friendly smile. She carefully lowered the girl to the ground.

"Welcome to the party," he said. "I'm glad you came."

She approached him slowly, pushing loose strands of hair away from her face. He was standing behind a beat-up old red pickup truck, in the back of which were piled many large sacks. He met her eyes, and smiled. She felt her heart beating against her ribs.

"Help me feed these people," he said, reaching into one of the sacks. She reached out her hands, and he filled them with seeds of many shapes and colors.

"I want to help, too," the girl said, and Zoe poured some of the seeds into her hands. Others gathered seeds, too, and began drifting back through the crowd.

They gave the seeds to all the people, instructing them to find their own patch of good ground to till. Placing the seeds carefully in each outstretched hand reminded Zoe of distributing Communion at church. She closed her eyes and saw them coming to her in a long line of beautiful faces. "The body of Christ," she said. "Amen," they said, gazing into her eyes in the way of people who know each other well.

The girl gave seeds to some soldiers, who used the stocks of their guns to till the earth. Zoe handed a seed to a group of gray-suited businesswomen sitting cross-legged on the ground.

"I thought," the woman who received the seed said dryly, looking down at it, "there was going to be food at this party. Gardening isn't exactly what we had in mind."

"Well, I guess this is a surprise party, then," Zoe said, smiling.

The woman rolled her eyes. "Why do we get only one seed?"

"Tend to it with care, and sprinkle it with water from the stream," Zoe said. "You might find you have more than you expected."

When they were finished, Zoe lifted the girl onto her shoulders to see the milling crowd that spread out to every horizon.

"Wow," the girl breathed. "Look at all the people."

And they're all hungry, Zoe thought, as am I after all that work. We've come too far to go home now, and there is no food anywhere to give them; just bare fields. She turned to find the gardener in the crowd. He was sitting on top of the pickup truck's cab not far off, and he waved at her as she approached with the girl.

"Children, have you found anything to eat?" he called to them.

"Not a thing," Zoe answered.

The man adjusted the brim of his hat and regarded her from under it, grinning a little. "Zoe," he said to her. "Turn around, and you will find something."

His words raised the hairs on the nape of her neck. Behind her, a great cry rose up from the crowd. She turned and saw not empty, muddy fields, but a garden, a garden that rose from the earth even as the people watched. Grasses and grains, vines and legumes, and every kind of tree that bears fruit grew up all around. Canopies of leaves spread out from trees as if to embrace the sky. Vines twisted and tumbled wildly around tree trunks, and squash and melons made low thunking noises as they plopped onto the ground. Boughs shook out the apples and oranges and pears gathering along them like roosting birds. Corn emerged with a green creaking noise, stands of wheat rustled and bent over heavy with grain, and flowers strew color everywhere. The emerging garden rumbled like an earthquake, and the people cheered and cheered—even the gray-suited business-women, who were dangling from high among the limbs of the tree that had sprung up from their tiny seed.

Zoe gasped and whirled around—everything was changed, even the people. Or maybe it was she who had changed, for now she saw the land not with her eyes but with the heart of her heart; and from that place, she saw everything transformed by love.

She saw the beautiful girl who had awakened her to all of this, and recognized her as Sulee, quite alive as she clapped and cheered and jumped up and down. Sulee winked at Zoe and began dancing joyfully; she reached under her nightgown and pulled out a long machete, which she twirled over her head like a majorette's baton. She tossed the machete in an arc away from herself, chased after it by doing two cartwheels and a backflip, and caught the flashing knife as it fell into her mouth. People applauded and cheered as she removed it from her mouth and made a sweeping bow.

"Isn't that a neat trick?" Sulee said, skipping over to Zoe and taking her hand.

"It's an amazing trick," Zoe exclaimed, picking up the girl and embracing her. "It's all amazing."

She turned to the gardener, and she recognized him, too; she knew him from the moment he had called her name. She smiled at him shyly, but she wasn't afraid; she only felt warm and beautiful near him. "This isn't Iowa, is it?" she teased.

"No, ma'am," he replied, laughing. "This is heaven. Come and eat your meal."

All around, the people gathered the harvest and shared it with one another, combining their simple gifts to make the best meal any of them had ever had. Zoe laughed with joy, and ate until she was satisfied.